The Persistent Widow Testifies

by Susan J Perry

Copyright page

© 2018 by Susan J Perry

First printing

All rights reserved. No part of this book may be reproduced, stored in a retrieval system or transmitted in any form or by any means without the prior written permission of the publishers, except by a reviewer who may quote brief passages in a review to be printed in a newspaper, magazine or journal; Printed in the United States of America.

All scripture is taken from several versions of the Holy Bible.

Susan J Perry
Edgewater, Florida

CreateSpace Independent Publishing Platform

Hebrews 11:6 But without faith it is impossible to please him: for he that cometh to God must believe that he is, and that he is a rewarder of them that diligently seek him.

TABLE OF CONTENTS

Chapter 1: Minister Joya Cannon   Pg 25

Chapter 2: Dr LaDonna Taylor   Pg 31

Chapter 3: Kathy Rasimowicz   Pg 40

Chapter 4: Susan J Perry   Pg 53

Chapter 5: Jeri Roberson   Pg 60

Chapter 6: Roxanne Lyons   Pg 74

Chapter 7: Barbara J Dadswell   Pg 87
        & Nicole Starr Barrett

Chapter 8: Barbara Wiklund-Maddaloni   Pg 113

Chapter 9: Maggie Brock   Pg 123

Chapter 10: Wendy White   Pg 133

Chapter 11: Nancy Herrold   Pg 151

Chapter 12: Emeteria Vega   Pg 157

Author's Corner: Pg 204

DEDICATION

Our dedication must always first and foremost be about our God, for He dedicated His son Jesus for the sake of the saints. We honor and dedicate this book to God, the Father; God the Son and God the Holy Spirit; the miraculous, wonder working God that loves His people. He is the author and finisher of our faith as we walk it out together we praise the Lord for this work. It is only through Him that this work is inspired and given.

This book of testimonies will glorify Jesus, the Christ our Lord and Savior. We are nothing without Him. We have no foundation without His inspiration.

So here is your book Lord, this belongs to You! Thank You for using us to write it all down and getting it out to your people.

2 Timothy 3:16 All scripture is given by the inspiration of God, and is profitable for doctrine, for reproof, for correction, for instruction in righteousness: 17 That the man of God may be perfect, thoroughly furnished unto all good works.

Thank you for all these women that you have sent to write their testimonies *to* glorify your name, Jesus. We love and adore you! There is none like you! This book is totally yours; we submit and surrender it to YOU our God of all creation. As you created the heavens and the earth, you spoke them into being. So shall we speak biblically here:

Genesis 1:1 In the beginning God created the heaven and the earth.

2 And the earth was without form, and void; and darkness was upon the face of the deep. And the Spirit of God moved upon the face of the waters.

3 And God said, Let there be light: and there was light.

4 And God saw the light, that it was good: and God divided the light from the darkness.

Lord we love you today and thank you for the opportunity to write.

FORWARD

This book is based on an amazing woman in the Bible. We do not know her surname but she is called the Persistent Widow and while we are not all widows in these testimonies, we must be persistent in pursuing God in all of our endeavors. Here is some of my research done for the pages of this book. Let us all be persistent now:

Perseverance

Defined as:

1. Steady persistence in adhering to a course of action, a belief, or a purpose; steadfastness.

2. *Theology;* The Calvinistic doctrine that those who have been chosen by God will continue in a state of grace to the end and will finally be saved.

3. Synonyms: tenacity, persistence

First of all if you break down this word you get a very interesting word targeted dead center:

Per-**sever**-ance

Per = by means of; through; each

Sever = to set or keep apart; to cut off from a whole; to become cut or broken apart

Ance = state or condition; suffix to make a noun from verb or adjective

Perseverance = the means of keeping apart any state or condition.

Bible scriptures:

This word is only used in the New Testament which I find very interesting.

Romans 5:3-4 And not only that, but we also glory in tribulations, knowing that tribulation produces perseverance. And perseverance, character; and character and hope.

Romans 8:25 But if we hope for what we do not see, we eagerly wait for it with perseverance.

2 Corinthians 12:12 Truly the signs of an apostle were accomplished among you with all perseverance, in signs and wonders and mighty deeds.

Ephesians 6:18 Praying always with all prayer and supplication in the Spirit, being watchful to this end with all perseverance and supplication for all the saints—

2 Timothy 3:10-11 But you have carefully followed my doctrine, manner of life, purpose, faith, long-suffering, love perseverance, persecutions, afflictions, which happened to me at Antioch, At Iconium, at Lystra--- what persecutions I endured. And out of them all the Lord delivered me.

James 5:11 Indeed we count them blessed who endure. You have heard of the perseverance of Job and seen the end intended by the Lord—that the Lord is very compassionate and merciful.

2 Peter 1:5-7 But also for this very reason, giving all diligence, add to your faith virtue, to virtue knowledge, to knowledge self-control, to self-control perseverance, to perseverance godliness, to godliness brotherly kindness, and to brotherly kindness love.

    I believe in all of these scriptures as we read there is an end result when we persevere. It is always a good result or a God result. In anything we attempt whether it be in school, at the job or in church when it gets difficult if we just keep keeping on, God will give you the best results possible according to your efforts and His will. I believe again as our words came the first Sunday we got together and heard about *endure* and *reject* that God works thru these words to get these points across to keep going to keep moving forward never looking back on the past as we grow stronger and stronger in the Lord. I want to quote the fruit of the spirit knowing we must have all of these as Bible based Christians who know God as Father:

Galatians 5:22-23 But the fruit of the spirit is love, joy, peace, long-suffering, kindness, goodness, faithfulness, gentleness, self-control. Against such there is no law.

    God is all of these and much more. So in order to follow JESUS, the Son of God we must be ever mindful of these characteristics. Do you have all of these? With perseverance we can be more like God and the end goal is eternal life and freedom from all adversity. People must know and recognize us as different, as precious children of God and this is scripture that Jesus spoke in red letters:

Matthew 7:19-21 Every tree that does not bear good fruit is cut down and thrown into the fire. Therefore by their fruits you will know them. "Not everyone who says to Me, 'Lord,

Lord,' shall enter the kingdom of heaven, but he who does the will of My Father in heaven.

So here we see there are keys to get into the kingdom of heaven & I believe perseverance is only one of them.

1 Corinthians 3:14 If anyone's work which he has built on it endures, he will receive a reward.

Our rewards come from God and not man. Our rewards will forever and always stay close to Him who is God, the Father, God the Son and God the Holy Spirit. No greater rewards are these for those of man are temporal but with God it will be FOREVER!

Any well known hero in the Bible is known for his or her perseverance. This is how we succeed knowing that God supplies all of our needs according to His riches in glory through Christ Jesus. (Philippians 4:19) One of the verses that I tend to remember often helps me through the unknown mysteries of God. It is:

Isaiah 55:8-9, 11 For my thoughts are not your thoughts, Nor are your ways my ways," says the Lord.
"For as the heavens are higher than the earth,
So are My ways higher than your ways,
And my thoughts than your thoughts.
So shall my word be that goes forth from my mouth;
It shall not return to me void;
But it shall accomplish what I please,
And it shall prosper in the thing for which I sent it."

These are the beautiful ways of the Lord that we can depend upon as we seek Him in prayer; as we seek Him on a day to day basis in all that our life requires…

Perseverance: It's a good word to hold onto as life rocks the boat of our salvation; of our Christian walk with Jesus and we must continue to hang on.

Reading & speaking the Word of God will help you to walk in victory as you persevere. God's kingdom is long standing and founded upon the Rock; perseverance is a reminder of this. Rock formations take years and years to form fully or to break down fully.

This book is about a special woman of perseverance…

This is a widow who perseveres, who presses in and pushed through until she's really going somewhere and she does it alone until she is helped. Every time we write a book, we have to live some part of it and today we go to a church with several widows. And when I looked around one day, I realized this to be true. God has somehow given my husband and myself hearts for the widows. It's not easy to be a widow but we serve them the best that we can and I pray we pass this test. Every book we seem to get a test. I must tell someone about this, so we will tell you the reader. Now I will be cognizant of the book title and the recompense of it each time I write.

Our God is an awesome God!

Special thanks to all...

We would like to give special thanks to those who have supported us here in this series of testimonial books because you are so special and extraordinary! There is so much love in giving. These women are putting their life stories out there into the eye of the public because they trust God and have received an urgency to do this Holy Ghost Book Project of 2016. We are grateful to so many. Here are just a few who have caught the vision that God has given us.

Love and blessings to all:

Dr Frank & Evangelist Karen Sumrall: A big thank you and hugs to Mama & Papa in the Spirit of God because they ordained us and believed in us above all others. They have stuck like glue when others have lost their connectivity. Only a few are called to stay close for a lifetime and I believe God has done this with the Sumralls and the Perrys. We thank God for them every day and believe in agreement for the vision they have. Blessings and favor always to our good friends...

Psalm 65:11-13 (AMP) 11 You crown the year with Your bounty, And Your paths overflow. 12 The pastures of the wilderness drip [with dew], And the hills are encircled with joy. 13 The meadows are clothed with flocks And the valleys are covered with grain; They shout for joy and they sing.

Pastor Pamela Ross: A good friend and sister in the faith of Jesus Christ. She is a picture of this woman which this book is titled for. She perseveres in everything she does for the Lord and just in life in general. Thank you for your continued friendship and prayers and with so much that you have helped to see us through. You are a true blessing from on high. We are honored to say thank you!

Psalm 61:1-2 (AMP) 1 Hear my cry, O God; Listen to my prayer. 2 From the end of the earth I call to You, when my heart is overwhelmed and weak; Lead me to the rock that is higher than I [a rock that is too high to reach without Your help].

Pastor June Wood: She is a persistent woman of God and mighty in the word and prayer! I love this woman! She always brings me in to her church to speak with her women's group and we always get fed with God's abundance. We are so thankful for her and our friendship goes deep and wide. Thank you Pastor for all your kindnesses towards us. God bless you with much love!

Ephesians 2:6 And hath raised us up together, and made us sit together in heavenly places in Christ Jesus:

Pastors Bill & Connie Sparks: You are such a blessing to our lives and ministry. We are always so glad when we get to work together. Connie buys every single book we write and Bill reads them. They are good friends and our brother and sister in the faith! It's not always easy to find such friends as these; God just connected us and knitted us together for such a time as this. Blessings and love to both of you, thank you!

Proverbs 17:17 A friend loveth at all times, and a brother is born for adversity.

John R Perry: Of course I must say thank you to my precious husband, I couldn't have done it without you. It would've all been a mess! You are the calm in the storm; the believer of Sar Shalom in our lives and I am so grateful to God for you because I know He sent you. I love your love and your beautiful heart and spirit, your prayers and the purity in which you see and speak only good things over me and God's calling on our lives. You are the absolute best Perry ever! John now is the editor; cover creator and producer of all our books and I am so thankful for him as we promised to be Team Perry for Jesus! Iron sharpens iron…

Deuteronomy 1:11 (The LORD God of your fathers make you a thousand times so many more as ye are, and bless you, as he hath promised you!)

Janice A Tidball: A very special thank you to my sister-in-law posthumously as she just passed away June 2nd, 2016 (on my daughter Suzanne's birthday) of that deadly cancer of the breast. She will be missed. She always read all of our books. She was an avid reader and never criticized in any way. She persevered living ten years beyond my brother Bobby, her husband. She is with Jesus today and I pray she is reunited with my brother who passed away May 15, 2006. I miss them both very much. Lives come and go but God's mercies are new every morning…

Ecclesiastes 3:11 He hath made everything beautiful in his time…

*** Testimony is one of the weapons of our warfare, like praise and worship: it reports the goodness of the Lord defeating any enemy i.e.: doubt, fear, rejection or any other name you can give it.

Jesus of Galilee

My Jesus who died on Calvary.
My Jesus who died to set me free.
Jesus who died, died for you and for me.
Jesus from Galilee.

My Jesus who cares for you and for me.
He shed his blood on Calvary.
He loves so much and gave his all.
Jesus of Galilee.

He is my friend, he's by my side.
He never leaves me alone.
He guides my steps in the narrow path.
Jesus of Galilee.

He came to earth to teach the Word.
He came to earth to heal and pray.
He came to earth to show us the way.
He's the only way.

So ask Him in your heart today.
<u>Please, Please,</u> don't delay.
He loves you so much, so ask Him in.
In your heart today.
Jesus of Galilee.

Elsie Counterman

January 11, 2000

Part 1

Older Women ~ Younger Women

God has put it in my heart to highlight this particular set of scriptures in the Book of Titus because it guides the women of the church. This book: The Persistent Widow Testifies is about women as they testify here to the goodness of the Lord through persistent prayer in seeking God. This must be led by the Spirit of God because he is our Teacher, our Comforter and we must decrease so He may increase…

Titus 2:1, 3-5
But speak thou the things which become sound doctrine: The aged women likewise, that they be in behaviour as becometh holiness, not false accusers, not given to much wine, teachers of good things:
That they may teach the young women to be sober, to love their husbands, to love their children, To be discreet, chaste, keepers at home, good, obedient to their own husbands, that the word be not blasphemed.

The church often has elders, spiritual mothers if you will to help teach the younger women to be raised up in the faith as fine examples to all. We must everyone have guidance in this life and throughout the Bible we see it's mostly a man's world. But women are being raised up in these last days to form a new pinnacle in Christ. We see women behind the pulpit and in authoritative positions in the church more today than ever before. This is an important issue in the church as women step up to the positions that God has called them to instead of hiding behind their husbands, their pastors or any other man for that matter. Now I'm not talking about rebellion or women's lib or anything against the word of God. No but to rise up to the calling on their lives and to step up boldly as the Lord deems fit battling against age old religion and slavery and prejudices, women are being positioned for greatness. We are seeing this more every day and agree with it in full.

The ministry of Jesus had many women in it supporting and following the Lord as He taught. The first person Jesus saw when He resurrected was Mary Magdalene as she went to the tomb that morning, she found it empty. Mary thought Jesus was the gardener at first until He spoke to her and then her eyes were opened; she recognized Him.

Mary was the first person that Jesus revealed Himself to after the resurrection. She was a woman, a woman that He trusted. He sent her to go and tell the disciples. She gathered them all together again.

When you go into churches today and look around in the seats the majority of the congregants are women who continue to support the ministry of Jesus Christ today; who are dedicated to the work of the Kingdom of God. God trusts them. He is raising them up more and more. We need women in the church of age and experience to look after the younger ones and to help with direction and good teachers of moral values and walking it out by faith. The Book of Titus pretty much sums it all up and I hope that our churches are doers of the word and not just hearers.

James 1:22 But be ye doers of the word, and not hearers only, deceiving your own selves.

Older women, and younger women are women equipping women, this one role of women of the church is to raise up the younger. This responsibility of the spiritually mature woman is important so God's Word which will be honored and passed along properly. This training of young women by older women to live godly lives is nurturing and spiritual mothering so good Christian women will grow up in the faith and also be good role models as the next generation of virtuous women comes along. Let us reproduce virtuous behavior among us.

How about Naomi and Ruth? They had a beautiful relationship so noted by the Book of Ruth in the Bible.

Ruth was married to Naomi's son Mahlon and both women became widows in the land of Moab. This city's name was taken from Lot's incestuous relationship with his daughters where sin took place and Moab is not known for its virtue. So upon these women's husband's demise they set out to go back home to Bethlehem to start over. Although Naomi had two daughters-in-law married to two sons, only Ruth stood by her mother-in-law after the deaths of all the men by saying this when bid to go back to her own people:

Ruth 1:16 And Ruth said, "Entreat me not to leave thee, or to return from following after thee: for whither thou goest, I will go; and where thou lodgest, I will lodge: thy people shall be my people, and thy God my God: 17 Where thou diest, will I die, and there will I be buried: the Lord do so o me, and more also, if aught but death part thee and me."

Ruth was determined and steadfast to stay faithful with her mother-in-law Naomi and with the God she served. Naomi influenced Ruth during these dire circumstances. The older woman helped to raise up the younger and then taught her to glean in the fields of her kinsmen; to provide for the two of them and later Ruth married the owner of that same field and many of us know his name to be Boaz, the kinsman redeemer (a form of Jesus) and Ruth was rewarded for her faithfulness. This Bible story is full of good news as God directed these two women's steps from Moab (the world) back into Bethlehem (House of Bread, House of God). This also types and shadow the salvation picture as well if you truly think about it. This is how Jesus saves us by taking us out of Moab or sin and brings us into His world or into the House of God. We must influence each other this way.

Another example of influential women who helped each other in the Bible was first and foremost Mary (Mother of Jesus) and Elisabeth (Cousin of Mary). They came together in a visit during Mary's early stage of pregnancy with Jesus and Elisabeth pregnant with John the Baptist. Both pregnancies were miraculous, both would change the world and salvation would come through these two beautiful women and their children. God used these women in a mighty way.

Luke 1: 41 And it came to pass, that, when Elisabeth heard the salutation of Mary, the babe leaped in her womb; and Elisabeth was filled with the Holy Ghost: 42 And she spake out with a loud voice, and said, "blessed art thou among women, and blessed is the fruit of thy womb.

These famous scriptures say so much about these two women dedicated to live for their God. They would give birth to the biggest changes the world ever experienced in any time before this or after. Salvation came to the Jews and the Gentiles and of this even I am a witness. These women gave their lives and the lives of their children to do the work of the Lord and will be remembered and talked about forevermore. Our lives will never be the same because of these steadfast women of faith.

Let us be women of influence and women of promise! God uses many of us for His purposes throughout the world in many nations and we should share our testimonies with others so they too may be encouraged to step out and go forth in the beautiful things of God. We are not talking about going to church every Sunday or Bible Study on Wednesdays but living a lifestyle that God sets before us. It is a journey into righteousness and holiness. Psalm 23 is a perfect picture of what God does for us and with us: A Psalm of David.

Psalm 23:1 The LORD is my shepherd; I shall not want.

2 He maketh me to lie down in green pastures: he leadeth me beside the still waters.

3 He restoreth my soul: he leadeth me in the paths of righteousness for his name's sake.

4 Yea, though I walk through the valley of the shadow of death, I will fear no evil: for thou art with me; thy rod and thy staff they comfort me.

5 Thou preparest a table before me in the presence of mine enemies: thou anointest my head with oil; my cup runneth over.

6 Surely goodness and mercy shall follow me all the days of my life: and I will dwell in the house of the LORD for ever.

Amen.

The Persistent Widow

She is found in the Bible by Luke 18:1-8, again without a name reported in scripture but her persistence was reported by a parable spoken by Jesus. This woman, a known widow had no one to state her case for her as she approached the corrupt judge again and again. The records say he despised the woman because she annoyed him with her continuous visits to his courtroom. He finally gave in and granted her request because she persisted with her pleas and disturbed the judge by this, not because he wanted to help her but because he couldn't stand her anymore.

This is how we must be in prayer before our loving and merciful God! If this unmerciful judge answered this widow how much more will our loving God in Heaven answer us? Our God is faithful in all of His ways. This parable teaches us not to give up but to persist, stay strong and believe by faith that nothing is impossible with God…

Luke 18:1 And he spake a parable unto them to this end, that men ought always to pray, and not to faint; 2 Saying, There was in a city a judge, which feared not God, neither regarded man: 3 And there was a widow in that city; and she came unto him, saying, Avenge me of mine adversary. 4 And he would not for a while: but afterward he said within himself, Though I fear not God, nor regard man; 5 Yet because this widow troubleth me, I will avenge her, lest by her continual coming she weary me. 6 And the Lord said, Hear what the unjust judge saith. 7 And shall not God avenge his own elect, which cry day and night unto him, though he bear long with them? 8 I tell you that he will avenge them speedily. Nevertheless when the Son of man cometh, shall he find faith on the earth?

There comes a time in your life when you must stop and say that's enough, I cannot put up with this anymore. It's God's hope that you would seek Him diligently, persistently and go to the throne of grace where you may obtain all the answers. God has them. His timing may not be your timing; His thoughts are not your thoughts but persist any way. And just so you know God never fixes any thing our human, finite mind way. You've heard the old saying, "I did it my way!" Well just not so with God. When He fixes something He fixes it right and fixes it forever. It is we humans that tend to mess it up always.

P.U.S.H. Pray until something happens and pray it always in Jesus name…

Part 2

Today's women are testifying now:

Revelation 12:11 And they overcame him by the blood of the Lamb, and by the word of their testimony; and they loved not their lives unto the death.

   Of course our whole object of this book is to glorify Jesus, I believe I've already said this a few times previously but can we say it enough because of the enormity of the deeds of Jesus. Second we would like to give today's women an opportunity to speak up and tell of their testimonies and encounters with Jesus our Lord. There is so much to be said as you will read here in this book the diversities of testimonies. Everybody's is different and everyone's is glorious as we come together to write and worship God. Our testimonies are a significant part of our lives and salvation. God delivered us from destruction and death through the death and resurrection of our Lord and Savior Jesus Christ. It is His name that is to be high and lifted up so He will draw all men unto Him in these last days.

John 12:32 And I, if I be lifted up from the earth, will draw all men unto me.

   There is a lifting going on here. As we testify to God's goodness, Jesus will be lifted up. His name is above every name and while we are testifying about what happened to us, we are testifying how Jesus impacted our lives and our personal situations. It is in the telling when we get set free of those things that have persisted within us, to plague; to bind us and to cause our lives misery. Today we let go of them and are loosed from this moment on as will you as you read the contents here. You may be shocked and dismayed and elated when the results of God's work is final as we the women of God become strong and persistent as the widow whom is portrayed in the book. She did not give up and her example is rich if you believe this parable is a picture of our faith and the durability of it. Carry on…

Luke 13:12 And when Jesus saw her, he called her to him, and said unto her, "Woman, thou art loosed from thine infirmity."

CHAPTER 1

MINISTER JOYA CANNON

"I'll never be the same"

It was an ordinary Sunday afternoon, after church in the spring of 2010. One of the members of HerStory International Ministries came up to me after our services were over and told me that her childhood friend she grew up with was in the local hospital on Life Support for almost a month. She said the doctors had already discussed taking her off of Life Support very soon.

I asked Sharon, "Do you want our Pastor to go to the hospital to pray for her?" She replied, "No, I would like for you to go and pray for Cookie."

So I told my Pastor I was asked by one of the members to go to the hospital and pray for their friend. He was delighted I was going, and seemed almost relieved that he wasn't asked. You see back in 2010 I was being obedient to a mandate from God to "snatch a woman out of hell" and train them Apostolically and Prophetically, to teach a company of women to live and walk in the fullness of Christ.

Jude 1:23 And others save with fear, pulling them out of the fire; hating even the garment spotted by the flesh. 24 Now unto him that is able to keep you from falling, and to present you faultless before the presence of his glory with exceeding joy,

Commissioning them to heal the sick and cast out demons and to encourage them to live as Christ lived and to teach other women to walk boldly exercising their authority in Jesus Christ.

I didn't realize it at the time that we had left out an extremely important element of Jesus' ministry at the time; raising the dead. Maybe the reason it was left out was a lack of faith, maybe on my behalf. Nevertheless, you have HerStory International Ministries. We met weekly for about two years in my den downstairs in my home. During that time we witnessed healings, deliverances, laughter, tears and growth. It was monumental yet, rewarding challenge of my life, teaching, training, preaching and exhorting women to be effective transforming Christians. Each time we met I always asked the Lord to endue us with his power so that we could demonstrate His authority in the Earth. I must say that God has been very gracious to us.

So, I accepted the invitation to go pray for Sister Sharon's friend at the local hospital that day. As we arrived at the hospital, we went to the Intensive Care Unit. When I gazed upon Sharon's friend "Cookie," as she affectionately called her, I saw all of the tubes and ventilator that was hooked up to her as she lay there lifeless and not breathing on her own. Sharon told me that doctors informed Cookie's husband that they were going to take her off of life support in two more days. To be perfectly honest, as I watched the machinery on her, I felt as though this was an opportunity to serve her as a rite of transition from this earth. I did not remember having the assurance of the miraculous at that time as I normally have when I went to go pray for others in her same situation. For a moment, there was a still quiet feeling of hopelessness in the room.

Nevertheless, we serve a God of Resurrection. Sharon and I began to pray, combining our faith, and then suddenly, about 30 seconds into the prayer, I had an impression from God to stop praying. What was this? I never had this happen to me before. Not knowing what to do next, I asked God to lead me and show me how to pray. I cautiously looked up at Sharon and I asked her if her childhood friend was saved to her knowledge.

Sharon responded, "On no, not hardly, Cookie is not a believer and has never been saved!"

At that moment my hopelessness turned into helplessness as I silently asked the Father,

"Lord, what should I do now, this lady is going straight to hell? And I can't stop her, she's unconscious and she has never accepted Jesus!"

As a burden of responsibility and panic tried to take over my spirit, I heard from the Lord who instructed me not to touch her body, but to lean over and stretch out my arms and pray for her symbolizing as Elijah did over the widow's son. As I began to mutter,

"Lord teach me how to pray," I began to pray a resurrection prayer over her lifeless body, which had no voluntary movement for the past 28 days;

Suddenly, her body began to convulse, jerking violently and her machines began to light up and beep. The nurses rushed into the room and immediately asked us to leave as I just realized we witnessed a miracle! Stunned and amazed I declared,

"God is still working miracles and raising people from the dead! Just as he did in the days that Jesus walked the earth, He healed the sick; cast out demons and raised the dead."

You see, I've always believed these things that were written in the Holy Scriptures, but this was different. This was tangible. This was real, this was here and now it happened and I was a living witness. To God be the Glory; great things He has done!

Fortunately, many years ago I had the privilege of being able to go to Seminary to study and prepare myself to be a minister. Yet, before that day in the hospital, I really thought I understood God. I thought I loved Him and had the mind of Christ. But, before I became an eye-witness to God's resurrection miracle was there a possibility that I was an undercover doubting Thomas? This was very faith challenging to say the least. But I wasn't going to let these unanswerable questions steal my joy, my new found joy! Yes, the way I believed was challenged that Sunday afternoon. Sometimes, God puts us in situations that stretch our faith and takes us to a new level or dimension in His Kingdom. He loves us too much to let us remain the same after an encounter with Him. Yes, now I realize that reading the Bible, being filled with the Holy Spirit, Speaking in Tongues, Prophesying and being used in Healing and Deliverance are all signs and gifts of Jesus' ministry. However, Resurrections are also a part of His ministry as well. I can boldly tell anyone that now,

"Jesus is ready to use you to raise the dead."

If He's using you in healing and deliverance, prophesying and exercising your authority as a believer, He also wants to get the Glory when we are used in raising the dead!

Since that day in the hospital, there has been a burning in my gut of dissatisfaction. I continually long to witness the raising of the dead. Ever since that day, I cannot and will not accept "Church as Usual!" I have developed a taste for the miraculous; I can hardly bear anything less. I desire to be a Carrier of God's Glory! I cannot turn back to a dull, lifeless, non-impacting routine in my Christian lifestyle. My lifestyle must exemplify the life of Christ. Yes, I am a living witness and I will never be the same.

Contact info:

Minister Joya Cannon
Impact International Church
Bristol, Tennessee

Covered by:
Apostle Ryan LeStrange
Pastor Jason Tanksley

E-mail: **joyacannon@hotmail.com**

Facebook: Minister Joya Cannon
https://www.facebook.com/ministerjoya

CHAPTER 2

DR LADONNA TAYLOR

My testimony…

I was born in San Antonio, Texas to a Christian family.

My grandmother founded 52 churches in south Texas and northern Mexico in the 1950's and 60's. As soon as I was old enough to walk, she would take me to stand beside her and hold salvation tracks for people passing by while she preached on the streets in downtown San Antonio, Texas. As I stood there I saw many miracles.

I was always taught that Jesus lived in my heart, but when I was twelve years old something changed. I was walking in an empty sanctuary when I heard the audible voice of God:

"LaDonna!"

I thought my dad was behind me a few feet but when I turned to respond to the deep male voice, no one was there! I felt a strong presence and realized that God had called my name. The next Sunday I was baptized and received the Baptism of the Holy Spirit with the evidence of speaking in other tongues. That same year I started playing the violin through a school program offered by the San Antonio Symphony. The first time I played my violin in church, I saw the same miracles that my grandmother experienced as she preached.

As time passed, I began to realize that the Lord was calling me to full time ministry. I started traveling and watching Jesus heal people all over the world as I played my violin and preached the Gospel. By my fifteenth year in ministry I had traveled over one million miles and ministered to several heads of state. A hunger for God and to stay close to Him is through reading His Word. My Bible has become and always will be a vital part of my life.

John 1:14 says, "And the Word became flesh and dwelt among us."

In January of 2011 the Lord dealt strongly with me to start reading my Bible much more than I used to. He wanted me to read 100 pages each day. Reading at that pace, I would read from Genesis to Revelation every 18 days! I have to admit it was difficult at first but I was obedient, not knowing the battle the Lord was preparing me for. I was going to need God's Word more than ever in the not so distant future.

In January 2012 a doctor made a mistake during a very common surgery and I needed nine surgeries in less than 90 days to stay alive. I was so sick that I could not even read the sign on my hospital room wall with the date and my doctor's name on it. I was in big trouble but I knew what God's Word said about the situation.

1 Peter 2:24: "By His stripes you were healed."

I remember the day my children told me what happened. My first reaction was that I would not let fear into my life. Fear is spoken of over 500 times in the King James Bible (my favorite translation). I knew what the Bible said about fear and I made a deliberate decision that it would not be allowed to invade my life. The things I was told were pretty frightening but I had a choice of believing God's Word or believing the facts. At this point in my life, I had enough of the Word inside of me that I chose to believe that I was healed and an overcomer. If you are in a bad situation now and are afraid, you can make the decision to believe that God is taking over right this minute. You can start saying what the Bible says about your problems and make a choice not to be full of fear.

I made another decision to forgive that doctor as soon as I heard the bad news. I knew that if I held unforgiveness in my heart that it would affect my relationship with the Lord. Even though the situation started as a mistake, it was compounded because the doctor concealed the facts. I didn't know how I would feel when I saw the doctor but I told the Lord that I forgave her and was careful to guard my heart against any bitterness.

I had to ask the Lord to help me forgive and apply faith that it was done. You might need to make a decision to ask the Lord to help you forgive someone as you are reading this.

With every surgery, I got weaker and weaker. The night before I was admitted to the hospital I purchased a condo in Alabama and was planning on moving in a few weeks and I had a very important television interview scheduled too. All of these thoughts were swimming around in my mind while the doctors were bringing more bad news each day. I decided to ask the doctors if they could stop the surgeries so that I could regain some of my strength for my move and finish my treatment in Alabama. I also felt that it was extremely important to do the television interview. I would have to fly to North Carolina but the doctors told me that I could travel if I was careful. I had about two and one half weeks to regain some strength.

My strength returned quickly once I went home. I was still very nauseated from medicine and was wearing a nephrostomy bag attached to my right kidney. My senses were a little dull from four surgeries in 30 days. There were moments when I thought that I couldn't make it to North Carolina but I persisted with the Lord's help and got on the plane. The trip was terribly difficult. A very dear friend met me at the airport and took me to the hotel. She also helped me get dressed and took me to the television studios. When we finished taping the show, the producers told me that they were very pleased. The next day when my friend left me at the airport to fly home, I stood alone and just burst out in tears and cried for a long time before I went through security to board the plane.

I was only home about ten days and it was time to move to Alabama. My son drove the moving truck as I followed in my car. I remember that I was pretty uncomfortable but the Lord helped me make the 10 hour trip. We spent one night in a hotel on the way. As soon as we arrived in Alabama, people from my new church were waiting to help unload the truck and unpack boxes. I was back in the hospital within five days. The bad news started again. I thought I only needed one more surgery but two exploratory surgeries were needed before the doctors could proceed.

Nothing could stop the downward spiral. Throughout the whole ordeal I remained so grateful that I had been reading my Bible so much the previous year. My spiritual mother (Billye Brim) would call me and encourage me to "practice the Presence of God." I would make a conscious effort to think about my Lord and Savior and shut everything out of my mind but the fact that He was with me and He loved me. Norvel Hayes, a dear friend, would call me almost everyday and make me tell him,

"My body is strong! It's not weak. My body is strong in Jesus name!"

He would listen to me and insist that I repeat it over and over again. There was a constant battle in my mind. The devil would tell me that I was going to die and that God did not love me like I thought He did. Brenda Kilpatrick, my pastor's wife, would visit me and make me feel so loved. Her visits were extremely comforting.

I got so weak that I could not read or eat. My digestive system totally shut down after the ninth surgery. Death was in the room. I couldn't walk without help and my weight had dropped to 89 pounds. I was taking strong pain meds every 2 to 4 hours. It was just a matter of time before hospice would be the recommendation. An email arrived to advise me that the television interview I did about six weeks previous was airing the next day. I had my nurse help me turn the television on and select the channel.

My nurse started crying as she watched the television interview and the Spirit of the Lord filled the room. The show told of my life and ministry. The Lord used it to remind me of my destiny. As I watched the television my smart phone immediately started beeping with emails coming in from people that were also watching the show with desperate situations asking me to pray for them! As I ministered to them in prayer, I started experiencing hope. I was reading the prayer requests of all people in horrible situations and praying for them. I remember how good it felt to pray for others and to pick my destiny back up. My doctors could do nothing at this point. Things were at a standstill for me medically. I was starving to death but I was still answering emails and praying for people as I became weaker each day.

A lady from my new church who didn't know me very well came to visit me in the hospital. She asked me about my ministry and noticed that it said on my website that people were healed when they listened to my music. She asked me if she could bring some of my music to the hospital and play it in my room. The anointed music created an atmosphere full of the Presence of God. I laid in the hospital bed weeping in His Presence. I felt like slipping away. It was very tempting to just get lost in His Presence and leave.

Seven days had passed since the television show had aired and I was getting tired of holding on to life. Tears were flooding my face as I woke up crying for God to have mercy on me. I asked Him if He would please send someone to help me. I seemed to be significantly weaker this day. Billye Brim called me that morning and said she was supposed to read a John G. Lake sermon to me. I struggled to understand the sermon. The pain meds made it extremely hard for me to concentrate and listen.

I remembered the last thought of the sermon. John G. Lake was ministering to a woman that could not realize that the Healer lived inside of her. After he talked to her for awhile she finally got it and her healing manifested. He said that the woman had Christ imprisoned as her Savior and had opened prison doors and permitted Him to manifest as her healer. The rest of the day, I told the Lord that whatever was blocking my healing that I opened the prison doors and proclaimed that He lived that He lived in every cell of my body and I was healed.

All day long I spoke out loud, "Thank you Lord that You live in every cell of my body and healing is manifesting! Jesus, You are my Healer!" I would not be quiet. I just kept saying the same thing all day.

When the day was over and things got quiet, I remembered that I had asked the Lord that morning for Him to send someone to help me. I fell asleep with tears rolling down my face and having difficulty swallowing because my throat was sore from talking all day. I had been asleep for a little while and my phone rang. I answered it and heard my pastor's voice,

"LaDonna, this is John Kilpatrick and God told me to call you and tell you that you are coming out of that bed and out of the hospital. It is your time! Today you hit breakthrough! You might not feel it and you might not know it but you hit it! Close your eyes and go to sleep and when you wake up its going to be a new day. You are going to fully recover! It's your time!"

I cried and cried and started calling my family and closest friends in the middle of the night to tell them about the phone call. I told every nurse that came in my room about the phone call. I even told the doctors.

My body started changing in just a few hours. My digestive system started functioning. In four days the doctor dismissed me from the hospital. In about six weeks I had gained all my weight back. My physical appearance changed so drastically that the ushers at church and some of my close friends did not recognize me at first glance! Doctors told me there would be life long medical issues. I am totally healed. None of the doctor's predictions have come to pass. I speed walk two miles each day and am stronger than when I was 20 years old! I started a full travel schedule about 12 weeks after I was dismissed from the hospital. The Lord has truly given me a miracle. As I minister now, I am seeing Him heal people that have been injured in medical accidents and some of the most desperate situations. He loves us! By His stripes we are healed! If you need a miracle, know the Healer lives inside of you and you are already healed!

Contact info:

Dr LaDonna Taylor
Daphne, Alabama

E-Mail: **drladonnaat@aol.com**

Facebook: LaDonna Taylor
**https://www.facebook.com/profile.php?id=10000939137
3554&fref=ts**

CHAPTER 3

KATHY RASIMOWICZ

A Vessel of Honor

I once was invited to a home church, and we all sat around in a circle to do an "ice-breaker" exercise.

The leader said, "Tell us something about yourself that no one would believe."
When it was my turn to speak, I replied, "I once was a head-banger." People looked at me with shock and disbelief as if to say, "You; A lover of the heavy metal scene?"

If you would spend time with me, you would think that I was born and raised a Christian girl in a nice Christian home with lots of family prayer and Bible reading, but that was not the way I was brought up.

I was raised a Catholic and had a general knowledge of God, but I never really knew Him personally. My parents would take our family faithfully to church every Sunday, but for me it was just a ritual. It was something I would call a "time clock religion." I showed up in an I'm good type of mentality. Though I do remember at age five or so having a strong love for God, even though I didn't know Him personally. I think because of this, the demonic saw me as a target and played hard against me in my life.

If you were to ask me to describe my life in one word I would say: it was "pain." I experienced pain a lot as a child; emotional pain more than physical. I never felt loved or wanted. As for my home life, I had good parents and siblings, but I never felt loved by them either. I was the eldest of three and it was evident that my parents favored "the boy in the family," then later, the late in life baby girl, my sister, both of whom I love dearly.

At school, I was severely bullied from the fourth grade on up. I never realized at the time that it was demonic activity to destroy me all along. I started getting interested in the occult. I started out with "harmless things" like watching horror movies, doing séances and levitation, which I learned from some older kids in the neighborhood as well as "sex games" the older boys played with the girls. I would take out books from the library on witchcraft and learn about tarot cards, spells, horoscopes, e.s.p., and the like. Ouija boards and the magic 8 ball were also part of my childhood and teen fun.

As a young teen I developed an extreme case of acne and my teeth were unattractive, and at times when I went out in public, my peers would be very vocal about my appearance. Pain and self-loathing set in, and I started to hate myself. Why couldn't I be normal like every one else? It is something how powerful our words and actions are. We can use our tongue to lift people up and also hurt unto death. We need to always choose our words and actions wisely.

I do want to mention something about this that I thought was most interesting. One day, when I was a young child, I was walking out of the church, and I noticed that they had some free booklets for the taking. I chose one and brought it home. I went in my room and started reading it. It was a person named Madame Jeanne Guyon. I was so overtaken by her story that I prayed that I would be like her. The thing I remembered most about her story was that she wanted God to be her only focus, but she was very attractive and loved looking in the mirror for hours tending to her hair and face. She prayed that God would take that from her. Soon after she was stricken with smallpox and when she recovered her beautiful face was covered with pock marks. You can read about her in the Foxe's Book of Martyrs. I stumbled upon this story in my later years, and I remembered what I did when I was young. It seems as though there are some similarities with my life and hers. I have asked God to reverse the curse that I feel contributed to the trauma I endured during that time of my life.

In my early pre-teen years I started sneaking alcohol my parents had hidden for special occasions and sampling drinks at parties the adults were drinking, and pretty soon after, I started to think about killing myself. I felt so worthless and unloved. I hated myself. I finally made the decision I was going to do it. I was going to end it all. I drank a deadly concoction of household poison. When I realized what I had done, my throat started to close. I ran out of my room to the kitchen where my mother was and I fell to the floor feeling my throat tighten more and more. I heard my mother in the distance on the phone trying to contact emergency. She said that I was talking in tongues briefly, which the denomination I was in did not do at this time, and I had never heard tongues before. Then blackness...Total blackness. At this point, I believe I died.

I will now tell you of what I saw. Now keep in mind, we were not a real religious family, and we didn't read the Bible so I had very little knowledge of what would be written in it.

Here is my experience:

I was with someone when I left my body, but I am not sure who or what. I was taken to a place that was total darkness. I saw images in the shape of people that were darker than the darkness. They were screaming and reaching, screaming like you would never experience in your life. There was so much pain and agony there. I know I spoke with the being that was there with me, but in that time in my life I only knew that hell was a place of fire. Later on in life, after being saved and reading the Bible, I found a passage of scripture which talked about darkness.

Matthew 25:30 And throw that worthless servant outside, into the darkness, where there will be weeping and gnashing of teeth.

The next thing I remember, I woke up and my Dad was standing there with me in the hospital. He looked at me with such pain in his eyes and said,

"What were you doing? Why did you do this? I just said, "I don't know."

I didn't tell anyone about my experience, and I just reasoned it away, thinking it was all just a hallucination of what I drank. After all, I believed that hell was fire and flames. I went to a counselor after that, but I knew all the right words to say and was released from treatment. No one wanted to talk about the incident, and as a family, we pretended it never happened.

At this point in life, I changed from the victim to a very tough teen. I was on a fast road to destruction. Living hard and fast, I denied there was really a God. I proclaimed that I was an atheist. I started smoking, drinking and quit school. I got pregnant numerous times and had abortions. I was living dead because at the time in my life I was under the influence of the devil. I shut God out. I didn't realize that it was the devil. I just thought it was me, but in truth, I was being influenced by evil spirits. I didn't care about how I was hurting myself or others around me. All I knew at the time was that it was all about me, myself and I. I became powerful the more I became evil, but in reality I was letting satan destroy me. I put up walls people could not penetrate. I just would not allow myself to care.

By the time I was eighteen, I was pregnant with my first living daughter, and I gave birth at nineteen years old. Now a single mom, I wanted to try and straighten out my life. I had received my GED at seventeen years old and I decided to go back to school, but I never completed and went into the workforce while trying to raise my daughter on my own; it was hard. Working three jobs and barely getting by; I still went out and "partied" when I could fit it in. I am so glad that I didn't abort her; she gave me the initiative to bring my life back to some sort of normalcy. I was tired of having abortions. I knew deep down inside it was wrong. The first one I had was when I was about sixteen or seventeen years old. I had a steady boyfriend then and we wanted to get married, but my parents didn't think it was a good idea and my mom arranged for me to have an abortion. My mom told me that it wasn't a baby yet; it was "just like a blob of liver." It was just made legal, and I remember it as a horrible experience. I didn't want to do it, but I felt that I didn't have a choice. It took a lot out of me emotionally, and it contributed to making me an even harder person.

Did you ever hear of the old saying, "Every knock is a boost?"

Well that was exactly what was happening. Every hard hit in my life made me an even harder person on the outside. Keep in mind that the enemy comes to steal, kill and destroy.

John 10:10 The thief comes only to steal and kill and destroy; I have come that they may have life, and have it to the full.

He was not only trying to destroy me, but everyone around me, including my daughter.

As life goes on, now twenty-eight years old, I meet a young man that would eventually become my husband. At this point in my life, I'm still doing the single mom thing: juggling life and three jobs while my mom helps me raise my daughter. The bill collectors calling and struggling to make ends meet, this new man, eight years younger than I, enters into my life. I am now so sick of drama and I am ready for a change. He and I dated and we got along just fine as we partied together. About a year later, he was leaving back to Florida where he grew up. I thought the change would be good with a promise of a better life, and I decided that I would go back with him. My daughter was now ten years old and I sold most of my possessions, quit my job, and set out for a hope of a better life for both of us, only to find out the contrary.

Once there, things began to change. My boyfriend became controlling. I had no car and had to depend on him to get around. It was a love/hate relationship, and I soon found out that he had a very bad temper. More pain, sadness, and despair not only for myself, but also for my daughter. At the same time, there were some good times and something made me hang on through it all, even when I eventually had an opportunity to leave.

I tried meeting other people, but it never happened and our "on again, off again" relationship continued on for about four years. If I only knew the word of God back then, my life would have been so different. I probably wouldn't be deceived if I only knew scriptures such as these:

Ephesians 6:10-18 "Finally, be strong in the Lord and in his mighty power. Put on the full armor of God, so that you can take your stand against the devil's schemes. For our struggle is not against flesh and blood, but against the rulers, against the authorities, against the powers of this dark world and against the spiritual forces of evil in heavenly realms. Therefore put on the full armor of God, so that when the evil day comes, you may be able to stand your ground, and after you have done everything, to stand. Stand firm then, with the belt of truth buckled around your waist, with the breastplate of righteousness in place, and with your feet fitted with the readiness that comes from the gospel of peace. In addition to all this, take up the shield of faith, with which you can extinguish all the flaming arrows of the evil one. Take the helmet of salvation and the sword of the Spirit, which is the word of God. And pray in the Spirit on all occasions with all kinds of prayers and requests. With this in mind, be alert and always keep on praying for all of the Lord's people."

Then my boyfriend and I planned a vacation, and he wanted to go see some of his old friends in North Florida. We would stay with a man my boyfriend knew from his childhood that was described as a "living terror," now born again. While there, his friend invited us to go to church. We agreed and when we arrived, it was a gathering in a very small room with maybe ten or more people in it. We sat up front and the music started to play. The Pastor, a woman, started praying in English and then began praying in tongues. Well, I got up and walked quickly out of there, crying, but I blurted out,

"I'm a Catholic. Catholics don't do things like that!"

At that point we decided that we should go get us some beer, but we couldn't find any since it was Sunday. Later, while with our friend and his family, I apologized to his friend's mother for acting the way I did. We then continued on with our vacation and soon returned home. Not long after that, my boyfriend and his friend we visited were talking on the phone. He told my boyfriend that things were going to change for us because he and the church were praying for us. He was right.

We soon started getting interested in attending church. We started in a Nazarene Church. I asked the Pastor what kind of Bible I should start out with, and he told me an NIV Bible. I went to a local Christian Book store. It felt strange there. I remember feeling like I didn't belong, but I pretended to be one of them and purchased my new Bible. I remember trying to read it, but it didn't make sense to me. The only thing I could understand and kept reading it over and over was something about muck and mire. I later found out that the Bible is spiritually discerned.

1 Corinthians 2:14 "The person without the Spirit does not accept the things that come from the Spirit of God but considers them foolishness, and cannot understand them because they are discerned only through the Spirit."

My boyfriend and I continued visiting other churches.

We both had a business together and we worked together selling and delivering shavings to horse stables. Close to where we would pick up our shavings every day there was a church that caught my eye and I thought about visiting some time. One evening as we were going by, I saw that they were having a service. I asked my boyfriend if we could go in and he agreed. Because we were working, our clothes were dirty and we just wanted to sit in the back and listen, assuming they would let us in looking the way we did. I slowly and curiously opened the door. There was a greeter standing by the door when I opened it, and I asked him if it was okay for us to come in dressed the way we were. The man was probably thinking of the scripture in the Book of James 2:1-4 that says:

"My brothers and sisters, believers in our glorious Lord Jesus Christ must not show favoritism. Suppose a man comes into your meeting wearing a gold ring and fine clothes, and a poor man in filthy old clothes also comes in. If you show special attention to the man wearing fine clothes and say, 'Here's a good seat for you,' but say to the poor man, 'You stand there' or 'Sit on the floor by my feet,' have you not discriminated among yourselves and become judges with evil thoughts?"

The greeter said, "Certainly," and tried to get us a good seat up front, but I motioned to him that I wanted to sit in the back. We enjoyed the service very much. The service was so much different than the church I grew up in. The Pastor was an excellent teacher and so interesting to listen to, so we continued to return and I began to bring my daughter.

As I recall, the Pastor would give an invitation to accept Jesus Christ as their Lord and Savior after every service, and one Sunday I decided to ask Jesus to save me. It wasn't easy though. In my mind, a battle was going on. As I thought about how much I wanted to do it, I also thought,

"No don't do it. It will only embarrass your boyfriend and daughter." Then I leaned over and told my boyfriend of my intentions. He said, "No. Don't do it. You'll embarrass us."

I didn't listen though, and I raised my hand and prayed the salvation prayer. Then WOW, what an experience happened! It felt miraculous! It was as if I went into another dimension, as if the weight of the world was lifted off of me. It was strange. It felt like I wasn't a part of this world anymore. It was wonderful! I was crying from feelings of joy, release and freedom. I was finally free, and God filled that empty void. My boyfriend left without me and took my daughter with him back home. I was invited in the back of the church where there was someone to talk to all who made a decision to follow Christ. They did this to make sure that you understood what had just happened and to give opportunity to confess that Jesus was now your Lord.

I remember driving home that day. It was amazing. The sun felt so intense. I honestly felt like I was in a dream or fog; some may call it "drunk in the Spirit." It was wonderful! I was changed in an instant! When I got home, I started throwing away everything I thought was sinful. I cleaned house! I also called my family and told them what happened. They were shocked. I also asked them to forgive me of every wrong I have done to them; God had started a process of cleansing and healing.

It was a bumpy road with my boyfriend and me, but soon after I was saved, my boyfriend was also saved and we were baptized together. He became my husband later that year. I am still praying for my daughter and believe one day she too will live for Christ. It's something how the devil can take our imperfections and make us feel less than human, undeserving of love or approval; BUT GOD takes those imperfections and makes us perfect through His Son, Jesus Christ. He gives us self-worth, love, and true acceptance in the beloved. Ephesians 1:5-7 says:

"Having predestined us to adoption as sons by Jesus Christ to Himself, according to the good pleasure of His will, to the praise of the glory of His grace, by which He made us accepted in the Beloved. In Him we have redemption through His blood, the forgiveness of sins, according to the riches of His grace."

God can take an ordinary, common empty vessel and turn it into a vessel of honor.

"But in a great house there are not only vessels of gold and silver, but also of wood and clay, some for honor and some for dishonor. Those who cleanse themselves from the latter will be instruments for special purposes, made holy, useful to the Master and prepared to do any good work." 2 Timothy 2:20, 21

God is no respecter of persons. What He has done for one, He will also do for you. If you do not know Jesus as your Lord and Savior, don't waste another day, for He says,

"Come to Me, all you who labor and are heavy laden, and I will give you rest."
Matthew 11:28

Contact info:

Kathy Rasimowicz
Mouth of Wilson, Virginia

E-mail: **rasimowicz2004@yahoo.com**

Facebook: Kathy Lucas Rasimowicz
https://www.facebook.com/kathy.lukacsrasimowicz?fref=ts

CHAPTER 4

SUSAN J PERRY

Perseverance in prayer...

The persistent widow portrayed in this book reminds me so much of my years before I met the Lord. I spent a total of twenty-five years divorced and single until I met the Lord in the fall of 1998. The first seven years I came before Him expecting a husband. Every prayer line, every prophet, pastor or teacher, I expected to hear good news. I was in the word daily as in prayer and communication with God. He had brought me a long way since 1998. I was single, divorced for years; three grown daughters all on their own and I began to really feel the loneliness of the single life grip me. I for all intents and purposes might as well have been a widow. I felt like one.

Do you remember the old television commercials that showed the old lady who had fallen saying:

"Help I've fallen and I can't get up!"

Who can forget her; she became my worry and concern of the future for me!

Ecclesiastes 4:9 Two are better than one; because they have a good reward for their labour. 10 For if they fall, the one will lift up his fellow: but woe to him that is alone when he falleth; for he hath not another to help him up. 11 Again, if two lie together, then they have heat: but how can one be warm alone?

Now this isn't really funny but this was just me or perhaps could be as the concerns of old age and thoughts of what could happen to me when I aged. As for many of us being alone, it is not a tasty tidbit that we want to eat and swallow; it's hard to swallow. In fact wasn't it God who created Eve for Adam in the very beginning of time. He created them as helpmeets and I reminded God of that often, whenever I came to Him in prayer. It was my utmost desire. Doesn't the Bible give us this answer quite sweetly?

Psalm 37:4 Delight thyself in the Lord: and he shall give thee the desires of the heart.

I had delighted myself; loving the Lord like no other; studying; giving; doing all that I knew how to do in the natural and the supernatural. I knew I had this strong desire to get married again and like the persistent widow, I went after God. I implored; I cajoled; I bargained; I vowed and I gave myself and my heart over to God.

One day I was in a prayer line at a church service and of course I was going to ask about my husband. The man opposite me, who was praying for people, suddenly looked up at me quizzically and said:

"Why do you ask for a husband when I am your husband?"

These were the Prophet's words from the Lord of Heaven. Well, I was stunned and shocked to say the least but nonetheless I continued on. For sure the Lord took good care of me but I wanted a physical husband who could stand with me when the world rocked my boat in any way shape or form. So I went after my request with a different tact.

James 5:16 Confess your faults one to another, and pray one for another, that ye may be healed. The effectual fervent prayer of a righteous man availeth much.

I knew prayer gave me plenty of opportunity with the Lord. I knew it would give me the inside edge and I kept seeking Him. I was the persistent widow when she plagued the judge with her requests; he finally gave into her as he wore out her faithfulness in coming back time after time.

Before I met the Lord; I was divorced in 1980 and everyone knows divorce is never happy or kind. It was very difficult and to be sure I was the biggest cause of it and so guilt and shame held me captive those early years. In fact just as recently as 2016 did I come to realize I was holding on to guilt and shame over my former marriage. A very intuitive Pastor prayed over me saying,

"The divorce was not all your fault!" I felt guilt and shame leave me after so many years. I never even knew that I carried this burden.

During my early years of salvation with the Lord, I encountered Jesus and He enveloped me in His true love and I heard His voice audibly for the first time saying,

"I AM HERE!"

He spoke loudly with a booming in my ears hoping the ear drums didn't burst because the voice was so loud. I suppose He was letting me know that His presence was there but also opening up my spiritual ears, so I could hear His voice. I'll never forget this moment, never, ever, ever!

I began to want a husband again; because from 1980 to 1998 I wanted nothing more to do with marriage, ties or anything else close to it. Now I could have a guy friend or a relationship but the "M" word was not in my future. I rejected this premise totally! I had failed once and I wasn't going to do that again. My children really suffered the most behind the scenes of our brokenness!

But God changed my mind and my heart. It has been an awesome journey but I became very lonely. God began to separate me for service and I often felt rejected and all alone. But of course I had Him and I was close to God more and more. I was at church whenever it was open. If I couldn't go for some reason, I was unhappy. I was at church so much they gave me a key to the sanctuary because I'd get there before anyone else, left waiting until finally they gave me my own key. I started opening the church up and getting things ready for service. But as this all unfolded I felt a stirring deep inside within me and had the urgent want and need for a husband. I had to get out of sin and know that God was God and you must get cleaned up first.

There were many scriptures I invoked and took to the Lord in prayer. I would guess some times the Lord had to laugh at me because I kept coming to His Throne of Grace over and over and I didn't often give up. I drew near to Him; I loved Him and I wanted only the best as I knew God would only give me the best. He was my Father; He was my brother; He was my husband and He was my God! Of course He is still all that to me and as I've matured, I understand much more. But when you are seeking Him, seek Him with all your heart.

Hebrews 11:6 But without faith it is impossible to please him: for he that cometh to God must believe that he is, that he is a rewarder of them that diligently seek him.

God loves it especially those who seek Him. He answers prayers; He gives all to us in abundance in the natural and in the supernatural. Go after Him like the persistent widow. I've always admired her to keep trying although she was battling a tyrannical injustice, she kept on regardless.

Giving up is not an option.

Galatians 6:9 And let us not be weary in well doing: for in due season we shall reap, if we faint not.

This is one of my favorite scriptures to share with others in my writings because so many give up before the blessing manifests. What are your heart's desires? What is it you have been seeking God for? Don't ever give up; God has a plan and a purpose in your life and for those around you. (Jeremiah 29:11)

I met my husband, John R Perry on December 31st, 2005 and I prayed 7 + years before I saw his figure. God told me He was preparing him for me. We married 5 months later on May 19th, 2006 and we are very happy serving God together as we promised in prayer. Prayer has continued through our marriage and daily lives to stay close to our God and love the Lover of our Soul. God has blessed us in so many ways. We persevered in a very special way as did the persistent widow; her example stays with us intently.

John and I serve the Lord today but we had needed so much inner healing before we married. We had been hurt and tossed aside but Jesus Christ heals His people. We went to marriage counseling especially since we had both been married before. We sat faithfully with the Pastor learning about a good marriage and we excelled through the teachings. We did what was required and it has been a great foundation for our rock solid marriage. We built upon the Rock!

INNER HEALING: When God heals the wounds of the past on the inside of you, He also heals the memory of it. He heals all of it. There will be no residue left behind. I know because it's happened to me a lot. So receive a total healing! My God is an awesome God; He is my healer! Persevere in prayer!

Contact info:

Susan J Perry
Edgewater, Florida

E-mail: **susiebqt987p@yahoo.com**

Facebook: Susan J Perry
https://www.facebook.com/susan.j.perry.14

Facebook groups: Holy Ghost Healing Book Project 2016
https://www.facebook.com/groups/466028446922987/

CHAPTER 5

JERI ROBERSON

My Testimony of 34 years of abuse; How God kept me and how he delivered me out...

I want you to know if anyone of you that are in a bad situation and the enemy of your soul, which we know as satan, is making you feel there is no way out with no hope of anything ever being any different; he is a liar. Our Father and Savior Jesus Christ wants you to know there is hope for the hopeless. There is peace in the time of storms and there is joy in the tribulations. You know the joy of the Lord is your strength and without God's strength we become weak and begin to feel there is no hope! So why even try?

We were born to serve the Lord. Every one of us has a purpose in life. Every one has souls to reach for God. How many souls will you let go to hell because the devil has you so bound up with your problems that you can't reach out to others. We have to pray, read God's word and fast if you want to get out from under the load that keeps you down and be an instrument that God can use to reach His people. Every one of us can reach out to hurting people. A warm Godly smile wherever you go can touch a heart that harsh words were just spoken to. But your smile warmed that saddened heart and made them feel someone cared enough to smile at them. I know because I've been that someone.

The enemy tried everything in his power to keep me from serving God; even to taking my own life. But all the time God was working all things out for my good.

Romans 8:28 And we know that all things work together for good to them that love God, to them who are called according to his purpose.

As a small girl I knew I wanted to live for God. There was a love rooted deep within from being raised in Church and having a godly Mother that lived her salvation in front of her 5 children. At the age of 12 we moved from South Carolina to Savannah, Georgia. My two older brothers had left home to join the Air Force. Now there were the three of us, another brother, my youngest sister and myself.

My Mother found a Full Gospel Church about 3 or 4 miles away so on Sundays here we all went to Church. We didn't own a car so we walked. I was taught from a young age to hold onto the promises of God till they came through, or I wouldn't have survived the abuse I had encountered later on in life.

Since I was raised in Church, I guess I thought I would some day marry some one from Church and live happily ever after. There were two things I wanted out of life

1) To live a good Christian life 2) And to be the best wife and mother a woman could ever be.

   At the age of 14 my girlfriend introduced me to who I thought was the love of my life. I couldn't get him off of my mind. After awhile he was allowed to go to Church with me. But I found out later it was only to keep me from dating any of the Church boys. He also hated the Holiness Faith. It didn't take long to find out he had a jealous and controlling spirit. I got a chance to go visit my oldest brother who lived in Texas with his family. I think my Mother was praying that my feelings for this boy would change after being away for about 6 months. But upon getting back home, he gave me an engagement ring. So at the age of 17 and he was 19 we were married. He was the only one with a car so I didn't get to go to Church as often. He had plans to keep me from going to Church. But I had plans to pray Him in, but I found out that God knocks on your heart but you have to let him in. And he wasn't about to do that.

   After dating him for 3 years, I found out I never really knew him at all. It all came out the day after we were married. He completely changed into a different person. He was no longer affectionate, because he said it made him look henpecked. I found out he had a drinking problem and women problems. After being married 3 months I realized I was the only one married in the house.

   So I left and moved back home, after being back home for 1 month I realized I was expecting. He was happy about the baby and promised to change. He thought that he had me trapped so he went on cheating and laying out in bars coming home drunk. I had been given a baby shower and wanted to get a little chest of drawers to put the clothes in, but to him the baby didn't exist until he could see it. So he came in drunk one night, so I took $5.00 out of his pocket to put a chest of drawers on lay-away. I thought he was too drunk to miss $5.00 but soon as he woke up he counted his money and came storming up to me and demanded I give it back. I refused so he began slapping me across the face but I never did give it back. The next month our son was born. Now I had something I could hold in my arms and love.

My Mother was diagnosed with breast cancer and had to have a mastectomy. I really questioned God, because she was such a godly woman. It really got my attention. I hadn't been going to Church as I should have because I didn't have transportation. God had a precious lady visit my Mother in the hospital when I was there and she promised to start picking me up. So I really sold out to God and to raise my son in the Church. That's really when the battle started, my husband said a son of his would never be raised as a Holy Roller. But I carried him and had him dedicated. The devil really raged because he knew a mother and a wife would go through pure torment to put God first and to raise her son to know Jesus as I do. This precious lady and her children kept coming to pick me up when my husband would go out to the car and yell at her,

"YOU BETTER NOT COME BACK AGAIN!"

When that threat didn't work, he just got physical and would push me around and hit me. So when I would see her we had it planned for her to drive by the front door and I would run out the back door. She would pick me up on the corner. We would pray all the way home Lord let him be asleep and most of the time he would be.

The drinking and laying out got worse and the abusive language as well. Our son was 4 years old now I felt it was time to get him out from under all the fighting. I moved in with a girl from Church who was having similar problems. We would pray together. So one night we vowed to stay up all night and seek God and a Holy Smoke filled that room where we couldn't hardly see through it.

My husband kept begging me to come back and promised that things would be different. Two weeks before the divorce was final, we reconciled. It was Christmastime and things were okay. Well I got pregnant with our second child while we'd been back together about 3 months, now he thought he was home free. So he started doing all the bad things he had done before and worse.

I remember when I was about 7 months along I had been out collecting for the March of Dimes in the neighborhood. When I got home he was so in a rage he hit me and I fell to the floor. The devil caught me in a weak state of mind. So one afternoon I took my husband's pistol and lay down on our bed to take my life. Looking back I can't believe I did that. But you can be abused mentally to where you really can't see any way out and no end to the pain. But by taking your own life you're opening up hell's gates to be tormented forever. But as I lay there on the bed I saw a vision of me surrounded by flames and the Spirit spoke to me to let me know I would give account for my life and the baby I was carrying. God showed me how it looked like. God let me know He would help me and strengthen me to make it. And He has. I have never had that desire again.

So our second son was born on his brother's 5th birthday and now I had two sons with the same birthday. Well unbeknownst to their father, I had him dedicated also.

I set out to pray and fast for my lost husband. I prayed some days when you could feel the power of God in our little trailer. My boys grew knowing what it felt like to have a praying Mother. As little boys they would go to the bathroom, when I would be on the floor crying and pleading with God to save their Dad. They would bring me a piece of toilet paper to wipe my tears.

Romans 8:35 Who shall separate us from the love of Christ? shall tribulation, or distress, or persecution, or famine, or nakedness, or peril, or sword?

I found out what it takes to keep going when the enemy is fighting; read God's Word, pray and fast. The more the devil raged the closer I got to God! I'm thinking of a song that says:

"Don't take my burdens or my cross away; for I would grow careless and I know I'd stay; my eyes would be dry and I'd never shed a tear; trials will either make you or break you…"

Well, finally my husband reconciled that there was no stopping me from going to Church on regular nights. But as far as revivals go, that was wartime. Whenever they announced a revival, part of me was glad because of souls that would be saved and renewed but I also knew it meant abuse for me to attend and he would stop at nothing to prove his point. Just some of the things he would do: He would take parts off of my car so it wouldn't start; if I got a ride with someone he would lock me out.

One night a lady came to pick me up and he was forcefully holding me and she could see through the windows. So she called the police for me. They came out and told him he couldn't hold me against my will. So when I got home he had the doors locked but my boys let me in. I got so when during revivals I would leave before he got home. But I would leave him a hot meal in the oven. But that didn't stop him. He would come to Church after me. He came to the Church one night and I went to the door and he grabbed me by the front of my blouse and scratched me all down the front of my throat and chest and told me to get home.

One night we had communion and foot washing in Church and I was away longer than what he thought, so he was on the way to come and get me. But half way home he passed us as I was riding with the girl who lived near me; we had picked up this elderly gentleman who also lived nearby. When my husband passed us he turned back around and came up beside us and ran us off the road. He jumped out of his car and came around and hit me upside the head and pulled me down out of the van and made me ride with him. The elderly gentleman just fell over on the seat and wept because he was no match for a mad man.

Another night I had come in from Church and had a bag of groceries in my hand and he called me from the bedroom. So I went to the bedroom and he sat up in bed and knocked the groceries out of my hand and washing powder went all over the floor. I went into the other bedroom to sleep. I remember laying down and waking up in a different place. It was a place of peace and rest; all night I lay in soft white clouds. I remembered looking down at the empty bed believing I had died and would never return. You can imagine believing you had died and waking up in your bed; but I woke up with renewed strength and peace. God knows just when to step in and give you whatever you need to keep you going.

Romans 8:37 Nay, in all these things we are more than conquerors through him that loved us.

I got news that my precious Mother at the age of 57 lost her fight with cancer and went home to be with the Lord. It was Heaven's gain and our loss. There was such emptiness because she was my best friend and the one I could go to when there was such a need. But when God allows something or someone to be taken from you, He doesn't leave that space void. He'll put something or someone in that place to fill that need. There was a precious family in our Church that took me in and treated me like family. God said if you give, it will be given back, good measure, pressed down, shaken together and running over (Luke 6:38) God will never fail you.

I went home one weekend to visit my sister who lived with my Dad. He drank beer every weekend. He was a hard worker and only drank on weekends, and he was a backslider. I told my sister that I left home and if we would anoint the refrigerator with oil and pray God is the Deliverer. I believed he wouldn't be able to finish the beer he had in there. We couldn't find any olive oil so we used cooking oil. I praise God it worked. He started going back to Church and married a good Church woman who he had known for awhile. They were very happy for years. Then he had a quadruple by-pass heart surgery and lived seven more months and then went home to be with the Lord and our Mom.

Awhile after that I was told just like my Mom, I too had breast cancer. I had to have a mastectomy. God is so good. It hadn't reached the lymph nodes so I didn't have to have chemo. That's been over 12 years ago now. All the time I remember back at the weeks of recovery; God used that time to renew my strength and make me even stronger in the faith. God is so good. So many women have to go to counseling after breast surgery but God was my counselor. He'll be to you whatever you need.

The year after my surgery my husband and I awoke to flames coming into our bedroom, our house was on fire. He helped me out of a window and went into the house to see if our son had come home. We stood outside at 1:30 in the morning on the 13th of November with frost on the ground and I watched our house burn to the ground. We lost everything that night but the clothes we had on. I lost my car also. And even God was working all things out for my good. Up till then my husband had all the say so about our money. He would give me less than $200 a week for buying groceries, paying utilities and bills. I'm telling you this so you will see that God can stretch your money also. So God got the glory out of the devil making it hard on me.

When I went to get the insurance on our house they put it in both our names so when the check came in, it had both of our names on it. When my husband got home and saw this check, he was furious. He wanted to know how that happened, just like I had no rights to anything. He was so scared now that I had access to the money that he stayed in a rage. It was so bad I told him why didn't we divide the money and go our separate ways. He said that he would have me killed before he would give me any of this money, because it belonged to him. I was offered a part-time job and again God was working all things out for my good. It turned into full-time with benefits and it's just where God wanted me to be. It's been a ministry within itself and God had already planted another girl there and God used us in so many ways. Well we decided to buy a trailer on 5 acres of land and things moved on. Over the years of having to do a man's job I hurt my back and even now and then it would put me in the bed for weeks. So my husband made the remark,

"I'll be so glad when you won't be able to leave this house

and you'll be in a wheelchair, then we'll see how often you go to Church."

Well, you better be careful what you wish on one of God's children because he became disabled to work from back problems. So he was up to his old self again. I was sitting at my dresser one Saturday morning looking out the window; I felt in my spirit something wasn't just right. I began to tell God how I had walked with Him and the battle scars I had from the abuse of 34 years of marriage. I started to weep and through the tears I told the Lord if my husband was cheating again, don't let him defile my temple anymore. By some miracle I escaped from getting any kind of disease through the years of his cheating. If God saw fit to let me find out or let the woman feel so guilty and call me and tell me she was seeing my husband: About two weeks later on Easter when leaving Church that night I felt an urgency to hurry home. Well all the way home my spirit was stirred within me I felt I would walk in on something and my prayers were going to be answered. But no one was home when I got there. But I still felt like I was going to find out something. When I unlocked the door this strong feeling came over me to push redial on the phone, but I said Lord I don't know what I would say if someone answered. But I was assured I would be given what to say. So I pushed redial and this girl answered and I asked to speak to her Mother and she told me she was out and would be back later and told me her name. The Spirit let me know it was her. So my husband came in later and I asked him if he knew a woman by that name and he said no, after hesitating. I knew he was shocked as to how I got a hold of that name. So he went to bed and I felt I should call back and she would answer, not knowing what I was going to say, I pushed re-dial and she answered. I asked her if she had talked to this man today and she said yes and she asked who I was. And I told her I was his wife and I told her that

I knew that he had been telling her that he couldn't get a divorce because I wouldn't give him one; but that was not true, all he has to do is ask. I told her that he had been cheating on me for 34 years and he could certainly have his freedom. So I hung up and this was on Mother's Day.

He came home after being with her and tried to sleep but sleep wouldn't come because she told him she couldn't get over the sweet voice that talked to her over the phone that night. The Spirit of God led me to push re-dial and to try and see if we could work something out. She told him I really must have loved him to live with him all these years and put up with his infidelity. While praying I saw an opened door and the Spirit of God let me know if I chose to walk through the door that God would be with me, keep me and guide me as long as I keep my hand in His. I saw His hand holding my hand and I was going around the side of a mountain and my foot slipped but because I was holding onto God's hand, I was kept safe and didn't fall. And that's the way it is if we will hold onto God's unchanging hand and build your hope on things eternal God will not let you fall no matter how rough the road gets. God will not fail you.

When it came down to talking divorce, he didn't know if he wanted to go that route. But he chose that route when he chose to cheat. So remember 8 years back when I stood outside my home and lost all my belongings; even God saw up the road where I would need money to help me start over. When it was all over he really realized what he had done. He called every week for a year telling me what a mistake he had made and how much he loved me and how he wished he had done things differently. But it was too late.

It has taken a lot of healing. I thought I could just walk away and start a new life but it wasn't that easy. There were a lot of scars and memories to heal and God let me stumble upon a song I didn't even know, it was titled:

"Pour Your Healing Oil Through Me."

I played that song every night for the next 9 months. Then I had another song which was good:

"What A Healing Jesus."

And someone gave me the sound track to it. I played that song every night and driving to and from work. And to completely receive my healing I had to go to this women's house, put my arms around the other woman and tell her I forgave her. I had someone ask me why I just didn't go and tell her off and take my ex-husband for everything I could get. I told them I'd rather God deal with hurts than bitterness, bitterness goes to the bone and can cause all manner of sickness. So a very dear friend invited me to go to a meeting where the Minister from Puerto Rico was preaching. He prayed for me and told me that I was ready to receive what God had for me and that God brought you here and brought me from Puerto Rico to give you a message:

"Oh such pain, oh how you suffered. I see you at age 17 (if you remember that's when I married); you have been ridiculed; been mocked; been humiliated and I'm going to heal your emotions tonight. I am your mate; you are going to feel the power of God like never before. You'll never be the same."

Praise God I haven't.

"Through it all, through it all I learned to trust in Jesus, I've learned to trust in God; Through it all, through it all I've learned to depend upon His word."

You know God promised he'd restore the years the canker worms had eaten up and He has. I married a man that treats me like a queen. If I told you how good he was to me you may think I was exaggerating. But God knows what you need when you don't. In my eyes I was overlooking this man. I was not feeling what he was feeling. I prayed God don't let me look through my eyes, but yours. You know where you want me and what's best for me. I hope I have stirred your hearts to know there is nothing, no nothing that my God can't do. I will close by singing "What A Healing Jesus." I love you and may God bless each and everyone who hears this song. I encourage you to read God's word; don't let the enemy steal what God wants to tell you through His word. You can find strength when you feel there is no more hope, when all hope is gone and pray because prayer is the key to God's heart.

Contact info:

Jeri Roberson
Savannah, Georgia

Facebook: Jeri Roberson
https://www.facebook.com/jeri.roberson.9?fref=ts

CHAPTER 6

ROXANNE LYONS

Testify, Endure, And Forgive…

We all have a testimony about the things the Lord delivered and brought us through within our life time. To be honest we should have countless testimonies because we are still here today by God's grace. Truly we can't count the many blessings that Jesus has bestowed upon us. Even the things we have and don't have know that God has spared us from. You may question,

"What is she saying?"

How many times has something happened that made you late for a meeting or an appointment? How many times has God spared you from that fatal accident when the red light stayed red a little longer? How many times have you been impatient with the slow driver in front of you, when God stopped that child from running out in front of you, or the deer from totaling your only means of transportation?

We must endure troubles and trials in our life time. Some things we go through we will never fully understand, asking:

"Why me?"

What did I do so wrong that this happened to me or my family or loved ones? But He is always there with you. When you cry, He cries with you. When you feel weak, He gives you strength, even when you don't recognize it. Some things that some of us have had to endure in our life time such as mental, physical, sexual, or physiological abuse could have literally taken our minds. What if these things didn't happen to you, but your family committed these acts? Maybe you're blessed and haven't had to experience or endure it, and the only thing you recognize is what you see on Life Time about a true story. Your heart goes out to these people. What if you encounter someone that has experienced a horrible abuse that you could never imagine, but this person gets on your nerves by how they act? You don't know their story, but you see the response it has caused in their life. So think twice before you decide how to react. You could wake up in their shoes. These things could have engulfed you to the point you don't even recognize the person you see in the mirror, or your mind snapped so much that you take your very life. Maybe you're enduring the same or a different battle and your thoughts and reactions are of anger, hate, rage and revenge.

I've encountered people so full of rage they blame the Lord and hate him with everything they have. Friend don't let this consume you, it's not who you are. The Lord did not cause this to happen to you. The person that performed that act of violence or abuse gave into that ungodly temptation of the devil or maybe even it's you who performed these acts. That person allowed the devil to plant that ungodly act inside them. It wasn't God who did this. I feel in my heart for this to be true; God gives us the freedom of choice in how we live our lives and serve the master as we choose. He won't force his love on you, nor will he force you to love him. It's your choice! You can serve God or you can serve satan. It's by your choice on how your life responds to you.

I just pray that when the Lord deals with you that you choose to serve Him. I will never force my beliefs on you. I just simply say I serve the Lord. It's by grace I am still here today.

So here is my life's testimony, and I pray the Lord helps you by reading this:

It was a family member that abused me sexually, and I will not say the name or go into explicit detail. My reason being I forgave that person a long time ago, and this person is no longer living today. I choose not to drag this person in the mud or cause an ungodly image in the families' mind of their missing loved one.

I don't remember much of my childhood, only bits and pieces. Some things I thought I remembered but were only pictures I have seen growing up or stories my Mother has told me. I don't know all of my family and some don't choose to recognize me because when I did tell, nobody would believe me except for my mom and sister. Regardless I love them!

My best way of describing myself throughout most of my life, I was very timid, easy going and eager to please people so that I could just fit in. Even to the point I would act, party, and dress like those in my adult life before I gave my life to the Lord. I never understood why I was like this as I started dealing with the abuses. But in learning from counseling on and off throughout my life and personal study and research I came to understand why I am the way that I am. This I learned that I allowed things to happen because it was all I knew, and out of shame I didn't know how to respond or how to act. I lived the innocence of a child wanting to please people. I knew what was happening was wrong, but now as an adult I let it happen out of the fear of rejection.

So growing up wasn't easy because of the assaults, abuse by men. I felt like such an empty space that didn't belong. In the back of my mind I was nothing, a nobody and my mere existence didn't count. I didn't even tell anyone what was going on, I just lived inside my shell. Growing up and in school the popular kids were so cruel and so mean, but I wanted to be like them. To me they didn't have any problems, not a care in the world and they were pretty. I wanted so much to be like them, walk like them, talk like them and wear the cool clothes like they did, have the pretty hair, makeup and pretty teeth. Instead I would go home and pretend that nothing was happening and tried my best to block out my life. When I looked in the mirror I saw someone hideous, I hated her. I hated who she was, what she was about and the life she lived.

At first I wasn't a Christian and I didn't believe in God or allow him to help me, lead me nor did I allow him to guide me. Well I need to correct that I knew God and of Jesus, but only in a small way of going to church with my grandparents and parents. Growing up through out my entire life I was in and out of church. In my lifetime I will tell you that I am now into my 5th marriage and lived in shame because of it being so many times. To give a slight description through out it I can say that I grew to know and learn the hard way; because victims of a horrible life are easily found and so very easily manipulated into thinking that abuse is the only way of life. When we meet and begin relationships we've already got that mind set we're going to be abused to the point if we do find a good person and in retaliation of being abused we convince ourselves that it's the only way to live and we are unable to cope with a safe relationship because we don't trust it.

As I am speaking to you about my testimony I would also like to add, not every druggie, criminal, thief or prostitute are a bad person. They have endured the same as you or me. The only difference is they turned to crime, drugs, etc. in order to numb the pain. This same pain that wakes us up in the middle of the night or you see someone that reminds you of your attacker, or a simple trinket or flower triggers that memory. These same people go through the same thing as you or me; they just slipped through the cracks just like the rest of us. Maybe some of us mimicked what we've seen mommy or daddy do. It's a vicious cycle YOU now have the power to change.

Finally several years ago I started trusting in the Lord and He has truly helped me. I absolutely give Him praise for it. It happened in what I thought would take a life time to get over in a short period of time. I felt the Lord dealing with me over my abuser and I had found out that his life was in really bad shape and I actually felt pity for him. I had this urge and an overwhelming need to get him a card. I don't remember exactly what I had written word for word but I do remember writing:

"Forgive me for taking so long to forgive you."

So I found out where he lived and it was in my mind to hand deliver it, but he wasn't home that day, so I left it for him. Friends, I am telling you that such a heavy load lifted off of my shoulders but I wasn't fully over it. Then more time passed and I felt the Lord dealing with me again. I felt him dealing with me to pray for him. That absolutely floored me, but I obeyed the Lord and done so. At first I will tell you that it really didn't come from my heart to pray for a man that literally ripped my family apart, because of being honest. So I continued to pray for this man and did my best at obeying the Lord, till one day I realized that my prayers for him became genuine. The Lord actually delivered me of that bondage and I was no longer a slave to it. Then the last thing the Lord dealt with me over him was this: I found out his health was really bad and I purchased another card for him. I had also gotten a prayer cloth for him and written inside that I found out he was sick and I was praying. As I went to church carrying the card with me I was thinking I could send it to him by a family member that started going. This family member wasn't there this day and I felt somewhat discouraged. Then at church that night I heard a lady give a prayer request for him stating he was in bad shape. My discouragement changed to hope and I gave her the card asking her to take it to him.

I will say that I and that abuser never spoke to one another and I rarely saw him. We never spoke, but I know God had turned what I thought my life was, a curse, into such an amazing testimony. I can tell you in all my past relationships I was so beaten down to the point when I did have a relationship that was good, I alienated it and ran because I didn't know how to respond to a man that was loving, caring and understanding. Then there were abusive relationships/marriages that the men literally used me and controlled every aspect of my life and existence that I had no hope. Throughout my life I have responded by making choices that my inner child would make. A lot of my choices I made I didn't understand why until I got into my adult years and working with counseling. The last counselor I worked with really opened up my eyes of understanding of how I was responding to being abused. I'm not sure how old I was when this person started assaulting me but we know I was very little. So the counselor told me at whatever age this started it was when mentally/emotionally a part of my emotional age stopped aging. Sort of like you hear people with split personality if you want to call it that. The child that was abused stop aging within me as I grew up. The child like person in me was in control of the choices I made when my life's foundation was cracked and broken. My inner child was continually in control of my conscious forcing my adult part of me to stay in my subconscious.

   The 5 year old inside me was in control. Matter of fact my inner child had thrived on fear, protection, and pure disgust. My inner victim held up a guard or shield toward many things. She was my guardian, my protector, no matter the circumstance, with no chance of negotiation. My inner child had absolutely gone into pure, sure fire defense, shear panic especially when there was a man in my life. For a short period of time I was in that fairy tale romance stage or you could call it the honeymoon stage. Then once I sensed the interest and desire of myself for that physical and emotional contact and I gave into sex. I went into utter suffocation, closterphobia. The only thing in my mind to do was get away, I wanted to run. Do whatever it was necessary to turn him against me. I had no concern over his emotional connection with me other than getting rid of him. To allow a man close to me made me feel that I had no control over my life. Sexual contact with men became disgust and filth. After sex I would run to the bathroom wanting him out of me, I would wash and wash. At times, not all the time I could see that child within myself curled up in a corner screaming get away because she was experiencing the assaults she endured all over again in her mind.

In my life time before I gave it to the Lord I can tell you what it feels to go hungry. I can tell you what it feels like to be beaten and raped. I can tell you what it feels like to be used so that I could give a man a son and have him taken away from you. I can tell you what it feels like to have to lay on your back in order to have something to eat and a roof over my head. I can tell you I know what it feels like to have a man tell you that if he wanted he could have me killed and get by with it. I can tell you I know what fear is. I can tell you I know how it feels to turn to alcohol and partying to numb the pain. I can tell you how it feels to be suicidal and in a mental hospital for 2 weeks. I can tell you what it feels like to be broke and not be able to afford the things needed or to be able to go to church like I would like to.

The Lord has helped me in so many ways in my life, also dealing with health issues by scripture which I will now share with you about the woman with the issue of blood out of the KJV Bible:

Mark 5:25-34
25) And a certain woman, which had an issue of blood twelve years,
26) And had suffered many things of many physicians, and had spent all that she had, and was nothing bettered, but rather grew worse,
27) When she had heard of Jesus, came in the press behind, and touched his garment.
28) For she said, if I may touch but his clothes, I shall be whole.

29) And straightway the fountain of her blood was dried up; and she felt in her body that she was healed of that plague.
30) And Jesus, immediately knowing in himself that virtue had gone out of him, turned him about in the press, and said, Who touched me?
31) And his disciples said unto him, Thou seest the multitude thronging thee, and sayest thou, Who touched me?
32) And he looked round about to see her that had done such a thing.
33) But the woman fearing and trembling, knowing what was done in her, came and fell down before him, and told him all the truth.
34) And he said unto her, Daughter, thy faith hath made thee whole; go in peace, and be whole of thy plague.

    Many times throughout different battles in my life other than the abuse and health problems the Lord led me back to the woman with the issue of blood with different meanings. What part I really reflect on was she knew the Lord was coming by her way. Knowing and seeing he was surrounded by many, many people she had to have fought her way through to touch him. Whether she pushed through the crowd or crawled in order to get to him she knew without a shadow of a doubt she would be healed. Jesus took notice of it and was pleased with her faith. Sometimes during a battle I feel as if I must push through to get to God. He knows our needs even before we do, but he wants to see what we are willing to do. Not all circumstances are answered then and there or how I think it should be, but I know he answers in the way he knows best.

    I don't want to just talk about the negativity and horror in my life; I want to share with you the times that the Lord has been there for me not just as an adult but as a child. One night I do remember at a very young age we had gotten home from church and it was bed time. That night was like no other night you and I would experience laying in the waiting to fall asleep. My room was dark and I was awake, then all of a sudden I'd seen in the dark this most beautiful golden arch with steps leading up to it. I couldn't believe what was going on but I wasn't scared I was at peace. Then all of a sudden I had seen a man with a white robe on and long golden hair. He would walk up the steps, knock at the door and then kneel and the door would open and he walked in. This happened over and over until I fell asleep. I never did see this man's face as I watched this happen but I can tell you the experience has lifted me up and stayed with me all of my life and I wouldn't trade nothing in this world for it.

A couple of years ago when I was hired to work for a dentist as a medical biller, my husband and I only had $78.00 left on our food stamp card. We were in need of many things and as we walked into a local market and I was praying to myself,

"Lord please don't let us go over what we have."

I panicked the entire time. When we went to check out our buggy was full, I kept praying and praying. The total came up to seventy-eight dollars and fifteen cents. I was thanking the Lord big time. But I noticed my husband Don hadn't swiped our food stamp card yet and when he did, it was seventy-eight dollars even! I could have shouted. Lord knows how blessed that made me feel especially knowing we didn't have the money to buy groceries.

So in closing I can say even though this is my 5th marriage, I no longer live in that continuous cycle of abuse that which was done to me. My husband is an amazing loving man that I get to experience joy and life as like I have never experienced before. To be honest things in life happen to us which are not fair and we question God, "WHY?" We all have the choice to choose life and how we want it to be, some of us fall under choices that people have made and it has really, literally hurt us and shaken our foundation. For myself I can say that I choose to live my life serving a God that can heal the broken vessel and put such love and forgiveness in my heart, which I will never be the same again. In my trust in the Lord he has taken what I once called a cursed life surrounded by satan himself, into a renewed life with just enough visible scars to remind me I am no longer where I used to be. So that little girl inside me that ruled over my life is now safe, she is tucked away in my arms within myself.

Now I am left with sharing my testimony in hopes to help others in saying you are not alone. There is nothing in this life that God cannot do. I serve a God that sent Moses to set his people free and parted the Red Sea. I serve a God that healed the sick, raised up the dead. I serve a God that became the stone that killed the giant. I serve a God and Savior Jesus Christ that can wash away my tears, put a roof over my head, shoes on my feet, food at the table, and forgiveness of my falters and failures.

Also in closing I can say, give it to the Lord, stand still and let God move. He will NEVER FAIL YOU, just TRUST in him. I was reading some passages out of the Bible in the Book of Job I want to share them with you. If you're lost I pray you give your heart and life to the Lord. If you are saved and at the brink of giving in and backsliding or you have already back slid, come back to God. He will help you when you feel there is no hope. I truly praise the Lord and I freely give my all to him, for he is my everything…

Job 1:22 In all this Job sinned not, nor charged God foolishly.

Job 3:17 There the wicked cease from troubling; and there the weary be at rest.

Job 11:12 Thou hast granted me life and favour, and thy visitation hath preserved my spirit.

Job 19:14 My kinsfolk have failed, and my familiar friends have forgotten me.

Job 19:25 For I know that my redeemer liveth, and that he shall stand at the latter day upon the earth:

The Book of Job taught me that in my life I will endure my cross and go through many battles but God will never fail me. I pray that this testimony has helped you. It's my heart's desire to share it and be a blessing to others, not for my edification but for the edification of my Lord and Savior Jesus Christ.

I **TESTIFY** because my Lord and Savior Jesus Christ has delivered me of things I have and will **ENDURE** in my life.

I **FORGIVE** because the Lord forgave me of my sins in life and it took back the power of my abusers had over me.

I pray many blessings and complete healing in every aspect of your lives. God bless you!

Contact info:

Roxanne Lyons
Bluefield, West Virginia

E-Mail: **Roxannec.wilcox@gmail.com**

Facebook: Roxanne Lyons
https://www.facebook.com/roxanne1974?fref=ts

CHAPTER 7

BARBARA J DADSWELL
&
NICOLE STARR BARRETT

Against All Odds: A Testimony of the Lord's love, mercy and grace and a mother's unconditional love as she stood in faith, walked in hope and trusted God's promises regardless of how things looked in the natural.

In 1991 I attended a small church meeting in Tampa, Florida where Evangelists Charles & Frances Hunter were the guest speakers for the night. At the close of the service Francis asked,

"If anyone wants a prayer cloth, please come forward."

So without hesitation I walked forward and waited patiently in line for mine. I wanted the prayer cloth to slip under my 11 year old daughter's pillow so as she slept the Lord could begin to reveal Himself to her. As I moved forward to receive my cloth Frances sweetly asked,

"Who is this for dear? And I replied, "It's for my daughter Nicole."

Francis reached for a cloth and started to hand it to me then quickly withdrew it. Immediately she closed her eyes, cocked her head with her ear towards the ceiling as if she was listening to someone speak to her from above and when she opened her eyes, she took hold of my hands and shouted loudly,

"Mother get ready... Nicole has a MIGHTY work to do for the Lord... Prepare yourself... Nicole's life will be a battle zone but FEAR NOT, God has 7 angels surrounding her and His work WILL BE ACCOMPLISHED through her."

Isaiah 41:10 "Fear not for I am with you; be not dismayed, for I am YOUR God; I will strengthen YOU, I will help YOU, I will uphold YOU with my righteous right hand."

At that moment I didn't know how to respond so I took the cloth and went home in a state of bewilderment. Nicole was a happy, healthy 11 year old living a normal life. She was doing well in school, she was a cheerleader for the local youth football league and she was surrounded by a group of wonderful girlfriends. How could this be life in a battle zone? Oh but little did I realize the magnitude of those words and how many times over the next 20 years I would need to STAND on them; and replay them over and over:

"MOTHER FEAR NOT!"

Fast forward to 2001…

What started out as a casual drink or two at happy hour soon turned into a way of life for Nicole and after several years it became clear to me that Nicole was severely addicted to alcohol and she was on a fast track to destruction. I tried to talk with Nicole and encourage her to quit drinking and to please seek help but my words fell on deaf ears. She would get so angry with me and would withdraw from me, sometimes not talking to me for weeks at a time. Nothing I said or did had any effect on her and I was growing weary watching my daughter self-destruct.

2008…None of the local recovery centers would take Nicole as she had no insurance and the cost to admit her were astronomical at $30,000 + which we couldn't afford but I was trusting God for his direction. I cried out to the Lord day and night and asking,

"What more can I do?"

And that's when someone suggested I look for a faith based program for Nicole. I had been running a small ministry for many years called "Angels on Assignment" which helped single mothers and battered women but now I felt the Lord was leading me to change the direction of AOA so immediately I began looking for faith based recovery programs. I had received my marching orders and I was on the internet day and night looking for recovery centers around the country and began to compile a list. One by one I called each center and asked if they were faith based and I shared my story with them explaining the severity of Nicole's addiction and asked for their help. While speaking with a director at one of the centers she told me to pack Nicole's things and bring her there immediately and they would care for Nicole at no cost. This was an answer to prayer so I called Nicole and told her, this was her chance to break free from the bondage of addiction that held her captive for so many years and it was time for her to begin her walk in freedom.

John 8:36 tells us "who the Son sets free is free indeed."

Nicole was a bit hesitant at first but she agreed to go and within 2 days her bags were packed and we began the long 6 hour journey to "Transitions" in Dyersburg, Tennessee. The staff welcomed us with open arms and as they began to explain to Nicole how the program worked and Nicole stood up and announced that she wasn't going to stay. Horrified I begged her to please stay and give it a chance but she refused and walked out. The director hugged me and said,

"When Nicole is ready feel free to give us a call and our doors are always open to her."

We explained to Nicole that this was her chance to be set free from addiction and without it we couldn't go back to living our lives caught up in the insanity of her addiction. It was time for us to step back, to LET GO and LET GOD begin His work in her. It was a long, quiet 6 hour drive back to Chattanooga and late that evening we dropped Nicole off at her apartment and tears filled my eyes as we drove away. I didn't sleep much that night but just before I drifted off I heard the Lord speak to me and say,

"Just keep loving her."

When I woke the next morning I was exhausted and a spirit of defeat tried to overtake me but the words "fear not" echoed through my head and as I began to pray and the Lord led me to:

Jeremiah 31:16-17 "Restrain your voice from weeping and your eyes from tears, for your work will be rewarded declares the Lord, They (Nicole) will return from the land of the enemy, there is hope for a future. Your children will return to their own land."

Though I did not see it in the natural, by faith I believed that His Word and I knew that his work would be accomplished just as He promised many years ago…

"Faith is the substance of things hoped for and the evidence of things unseen." Hebrews 11:1.

I took a deep breath and with a sense of purpose I sat at my computer and began to set up a website that listed all the faith based centers I had spoken with. I listed what the requirements were, length of stay, costs, etc. Just because my daughter wouldn't go into a recovery program I was still going to be obedient to the Lord and do all I could to help lead others to a program that they too so desperately needed. Hence the beginning of AOAMINISTRY.com was birthed.

I had hoped that Nicole would call and tell me she had made a mistake but that was wishful thinking. Weeks passed with no communication with her so I did what I needed to do and I stood in the gap and prayed over her day and night. I prayed and asked God,

"Please Lord, send a stranger to Nicole's door; please send someone to her that can reach her at her point of need."

Days turned into months and then into years and Nicole was in and out of hospital emergency rooms over 50 times. She was admitted to ICU over and over again and the doctor's kept telling her she had to quit drinking or she was going to die. Nothing anyone said seemed to have any effect on her but I continued to pray and asked God to please wake her from her slumber and show Himself to her.

I was trying to regain a sense of normal in my life so when an invitation came for me to attend a 3 day Christian retreat in March of 2010 I gladly accepted. I really needed some time away to rest, relax and recharge my batteries and in the weeks prior to that invitation God began speaking to me about letting go of Nicole and turn her over to Him completely. In my spirit I heard the Lord tell me to read:

Ephesians 6:12-18 For your struggle is not against flesh and blood, but against the rulers, against the authorities, against the powers of this dark world and against the spiritual forces of evil in the heavenly realms. Therefore put on the full armour of God, so that when the days of evil come, you may be able to stand your ground, and after you have dome everything, STAND...

I arrived at my weekend retreat and they handed me my name badge with the weekend's theme printed in big, bold letters. It was the word: **STAND.** I had done all that I could in the natural for Nicole and it was time to step back and **STAND.** This was no coincidence, it was God getting me ready, He was preparing me for what was ahead so I took a deep breath and I was ready for the ride of my life...

At one point in the weekend we were asked to write something down that we were holding back from God and nail it to the cross in complete surrender. I thought a moment and immediately a slide show played before my eyes... God showed me that every time I laid Nicole before the Lord and just before I would turn to walk away I would pinch off a tiny speck and tuck her in my pocket just in case God needed my help. He spoke clearly to me that day and said:

"Release her to ME completely and watch what I can do."

As I left the retreat that weekend I knew in my spirit that something was going to happen and I just needed to trust God. And sure enough, 3 days later on March 10, 2010 the telephone rang at 5:45 AM. My first thought was Nicole had been rushed to the emergency room again and I would be needed at the hospital. But no, a clear, calm voice spoke to me and said,

"Mom, I don't know if I did it right but I asked Jesus to come into my life. When I was sleeping I heard a song playing and when I woke up I saw Jesus standing in my room with His hand stretched out towards me. I thought He had come to tell me my time was up. I sat up and cried out, 'I DON'T WANT TO DIE; I have something I'm supposed to do for you. Jesus please help me.'"

WOW, as quickly as I had released Nicole fully to His care He immediately began moving in her life. Tears of joy filled my eyes and I thanked Him for hearing her cry for help and for hearing the cries of her praying mother. I sang praises all day long knowing that Nicole was born again and she had received the gift of eternal life. But within a matter of days the enemy came calling. He came to instill doubt and unbelief in Nicole and before long she was caught back in his web and was drinking once again. Nicole was saved but the stronghold of addiction still had its ugly grip on her and there was no one other than me who came up alongside of Nicole to help nurture her and strengthen her in her new walk and as I spoke words of truth, again she went running.

This went on for 2 more years and trips back and forth to the hospital and each report was getting worse and worse but I had given Nicole over to the Lord and I made a promise not to take the problem back. So on the side lines I suited up just as the Word told me and I started warring in the spirit realm on her behalf.

"The weapons of our warfare are not carnal but mighty through God to the pulling down of strongholds." 2 Corinthians 10:4

I was trusting God and I held Him at His Word and I prayed,

"Dear Lord, do whatever it takes but PLEASE spare my daughter's life!"

It was now 2012 and the addiction had taken its toll and Nicole's body was shutting down and was showing tremendous signs of her illness. Her abdomen was full of fluid, her skin was greenish-yellow and her eyes were the color of Big Bird. She withdrew from me more and more and refused to let me see her or take her to the hospital. I knew it was going to take a miracle to get through to her and I was to trust God to move on her behalf.

I had recently heard about a local church in Chattanooga that had an amazing ministry working with substance abuse recovery so I felt led to go and seek their help. I was introduced to Pastor Frank and his brother Pastor John and I shared my story with them. Without knowing me Pastor John said that he would go with me to speak to Nicole. As he was knocking on her door I heard the still small voice of the Lord say:

"I heard your prayers when you asked for a stranger to come to her door."

A smile came across my face and I knew the LORD was right there with us. Slowly the door opened and Nicole peeked out to see who it was. As we entered her apartment Pastor John smiled and introduced himself. He held her hands and without any judgment he said he was there to help and asked if she would agree to go to the hospital to get some medical help. Without hesitation Nicole looked him in the eyes and said, "YES." As she went into her room to get ready Pastor John told me that Nicole was in the worst condition that he had ever seen in his 15 years of doing recovery work so we quickly got Nicole in the car and we headed off to the emergency room. After hours of tests the doctor walked into the room and spoke the words that no mother wants to hear:

"Nicole is in end stage liver failure and there's not much more we can do for her."

So once again she was admitted to ICU to help stabilize her and all the while they kept telling me:

"It's just going to be a matter of time."

Nicole was discharged a few days later and the reality of what was happening within her body still hadn't sunk in. She had previously made plans to go camping at the lake with some friends and I tried to discourage her and I asked her to please come home with me so I could take care of her but she told me she would be okay and she would come home soon. It was a typical southern summer's day, extremely hot and humid with no relief from the heat except for air conditioning and here she was a sick young woman heading off to go camping in a tent. After a few days Nicole called me to say she wasn't feeling well and asked if she could come back home. Without hesitation I accepted her with open arms...

The prodigal was coming home and just as the Lord had spoken to me, I kept loving her. She told me she felt like she was going to pass out and I asked her where she was. She said:

"I'm at Skull Island Campground."

How apropos a name for what was about to unfold; I grabbed my keys and flew out the door. The entire way I prayed in the spirit and I was pleading the blood of Jesus over her. Repeatedly my cell phone would ring and she asked:

"Mom where are you? Please get here soon, I need you here now."

Nicole knew that no matter what I loved her unconditionally and I would do whatever I could for her good and I told her to hold on I'm on my way. As I pulled into the campground I saw several tents but no sign of Nicole anywhere. I began running between the tents calling out her name and I heard her tiny voice cry out:

"Mom I'm in here."

As I entered the tent I wasn't prepared for what I saw. There she lay on an air mattress covered with blood, bruises all over her body and she was so weak she couldn't even stand up. I screamed for someone, anyone to come help me get Nicole into my car and a neighboring camper ran to my aid. I called my husband and told him to meet us at the emergency room ASAP…

On the way there I reminded Nicole that she is a child of God and that HE has His hand upon her and the word of promise that He spoke through Frances those many years ago would not come back void and she faintly whispered,

"I know Mom."

We bypassed the formalities of check in at the ER when they saw Nicole's condition and immediately they began treating her with IVs as they prepared her for transfer to their main campus. Nicole was bleeding internally with 5 esophageal bleeds and because of the severity of her liver damage Nicole had no clotting factor and she had a hematoma the size of a serving platter across her lower back. I followed the ambulance downtown and was told to stay in the waiting area. She was in critical condition and they were unsure if she was going to make it, they said the prognosis was not promising. At that moment the voice of the Lord spoke to me in a shout and said:

"I have given you the keys to the Kingdom of Heaven and what you bind on earth will be bound in heaven."

From deep within me like a roaring lion protecting her cub I bound the spirit of bondage and infirmity and commanded it to once and for all loose Nicole and let her go. I put the enemy on notice and shouted:

"She is covered by the blood of Jesus…satan you MUST take your filthy hands off of her."

A new boldness came over me that day and I became a warrior and I prayed like I had never prayed before. Thankfully I had just finished reading Judy Jacobs book: Take it By Force, Faith that Stands Firm in the Face of Opposition; and deep within my heart I knew Nicole would make it and again I heard the Lord say;

"Mother, FEAR NOT."

I walked the halls outside of the operating room praying and playing Christian music and filling the atmosphere with songs of praise and worship and 2 hours later they came and said they had moved Nicole to ICU. The Dr. pulled my husband aside and said prepare your wife for the worst, Nicole is on life support with little hope for recovery but death was not an option I was trusting God and I cried out to Jehovah Rapha our Healer and I spoke words of life over her body.

Psalm 118:16-17 "Nicole, you will live and not die and together we will declare the mighty works of the Lord."

I was believing by faith that He would complete the good work He began in her. Philippians 1:6

Within days Nicole was sitting up and eating so they said she was ready to go home. Elated by the amazing turn around I brought Nicole home and I became her full time caregiver. One morning when she woke she said,

"Mom, when I was sleeping I heard a voice and it kept saying, "JOB....JOB....JOB..."

A smile came to me and I told her that God was letting her know that He is with you and as Job 42:2 says:

"No plan of God's can be thwarted."

For the next few days all was well but on day 5 I noticed Nicole was acting different, she had stopped eating and wasn't drinking anything. Her coloring was different; she glowed like a yellow highlighter and when I spoke to her she looked right through me. I called a friend who is a nurse and asked if she could come by the house for a few minutes, I sensed in my spirit that something was terribly wrong with Nicole. Within seconds of her arriving Nicole sat up in bed and vomited a fountain of blood. Mina jumped into action attending to Nicole and shouted,

"Call 911."

When the EMTs arrived and saw the tremendous blood loss they said Nicole wasn't going to make it to the hospital but I shouted back:

"God has His hand upon her and she's going to make it."

I asked to ride in the ambulance with her and they said it wasn't allowed but I wasn't going to leave Nicole's side and I fell on my knees and I prayed:

"Please Lord, don't take my little girl. Make a way where there seems to be no way.

The EMTs quickly loaded Nicole into the ambulance and at the last minute they shouted,

"Jump in the front seat and let's go."

I prayed in the spirit the whole way down the mountain pleading the precious healing blood of Jesus over her and just as we pulled up to the hospital emergency room I heard

Nicole cough from the back of the ambulance. I knew God was with us and He wasn't through with her yet...

Psalm 31:22 "You heard my cry for mercy when I called to you for help."

A doctor who wasn't scheduled to work the ER that afternoon just happened to be filling in for a colleague. He jumped on the scene and began barking orders to the ER staff. Nicole had lost 50% of her blood and her pressure had dropped to 40/37. Like bees flying over a honey pot there were doctors and nurses everywhere working to keep Nicole alive. Again she was rushed into surgery to find the cause for the blood loss and she was back on life support and 10 more days in the hospital. But still, I kept focused on God's Word and I wrote healing scriptures on index cards and taped them around her room. I wrapped Nicole in my Tallit (prayer shawl) and I wove the wings (the tassels) through her fingers. Just as the woman with the issue of blood who pressed in to touch the hem (tassels) of Jesus' garment I pressed in and stood in the gap for Nicole. God is no respecter of persons and what He did for that woman I was claiming for Nicole...

Luke 8:48 "Daughter be of good cheer, it is by faith that she is made well."

Days later Nicole was transferred to a private room and a delivery of flowers arrived with them came a small brown teddy bear. I did everything I could to make Nicole comfortable and I did whatever I could to try and make her smile. I grabbed the teddy bear from the box and with his small fuzzy face I began giving her teddy bear kisses all over her cheeks. This tiny bear had brought a smile to Nicole's face, a smile that I hadn't seen in a long time so I grabbed him again and began kissing her and speaking words of hope to her. Immediately the teddy bear took on a life of his own and Nicole whispered,

"Mom, what's his name?" Without hesitation I said, "We'll name him RAPHA for Jehovah Rapha your healer and from that moment on "Rapha Bear" never left her side. He was her constant companion, her point of contact to the Lord...

Again there was talk of releasing Nicole to come back home but this time I needed help and support in caring for her. Almost every friend that we had in our life dropped out one by one and walked away when we needed them the most. You see ministry is messy and people don't want to get their hands dirty but I had a dear friend in Florida that I called and asked if she would come to Tennessee and help me with Nicole. Without hesitation my friend Nanette agreed and within 3 days she was there by our side.

Nicole was home for 3 days then back to the hospital for 5 days; back home for 2 days and back to the ER. But no matter where we were "Rapha Bear" was always at Nicole's side and she knew that the Lord was right there with her. Hospital visits went on for months and every doctor and nurse that came into our room and gave us reports of doom and gloom. They all said it was impossible for Nicole to be considered for a liver transplant and there really wasn't anything more they could do for her. Each day I would declare God's Word over her and I wasn't taking no for an answer.

Matthew 19:26 "with men this is impossible but with God all things are possible."

Something stirred in my spirit and I knew I had to get another opinion so I moved Nicole to another local hospital and sure enough by divine appointment Nicole was in care of an amazing liver specialist who just happened to be on rounds that day. Seeing the severity of her case Dr. Patel began to make plans for a transfer to Vanderbilt Hospital in Nashville, TN where they did liver transplants, but there was one thing holding Nicole back from being transferred. Nicole needed her Medicaid # which we had applied for months before and her paperwork was stalled somewhere in the system. How could we speed up the process? My husband suggested we call our Senator and explain the urgency of our case to him but how could we get an audience with the Senator? I kept in touch with Pastor John and updated him on Nicole's condition and I explained our dilemma to him and our thoughts of trying to reach the Senator and he said,

"There just happens to be a member of our church that works for the Senator and I'll give him a call now."

Before we knew it they were working on Nicole's behalf to rush her paperwork through the system. This truly was divine favor from above. Time was ticking away for Nicole and I stood by her bedside day and night praying for a miracle to take place. The very next day Nicole's nurse rushed in and said they were transporting her by ambulance and she would be heading off to Vanderbilt immediately. We were asked to wait until morning to head over there because of the late hour so we went home to rest and prepare for the days ahead. As I lay in bed that night in my husband's arms crying so hard I could barely talk, I told him,

"I can't explain it to anyone but I know in my heart that Nicole is going to make it. I know that God is faithful to His Word."

We arrived at Vanderbilt Hospital early the next morning and we were greeted by a team of doctors. They told us that Nicole had a seizure in the early morning hours and she had several bleeds in her brain, she was on life support. Additionally, she was now in kidney failure and they had her on 24 hour bedside dialysis. The head of MICU and the head liver transplant doctor pulled me aside and said I needed to brace myself for the worst as Nicole was not expected to wake up. Once again it was time to set the record straight so I poked my finger in the doctor's chest and I said,

"NO, God has His hand upon Nicole and she will live and not die. Nicole will wake up so please, when you talk about Nicole, say when she wakes up."

Mark 11:23 "If anyone says to this mountain, go throw yourself into the sea; and does not doubt in his heart but believes what he says will happen, it will be done for them."

We stayed by her side throughout the day and with Rapha Bear tucked under her arm and we prayed over her continuously telling her it was time to wake up…

Malachi 4:2 says: "But you Nicole, a daughter of righteousness shall arise, there is healing in His wings."

By noon Nicole's toes began to wiggle, by 5 PM she was squeezing my hand and at 8 PM her eyes popped open… Nicole was awake. I ran into the hallway and called the nurse and when the doctors came in the room they studied the monitors and whispered amongst themselves. One of the doctors looked over at me and I smiled and said,

"I told you God has His hand on her."

Within days they were discharging her out of MICU calling her their star patient and they moved her into a private room which we thought was a good sign but as the days went on Nicole's blood pressure once again was dropping to extreme lows. She was getting blood transfusions almost daily and she continued on a rigorous dialysis schedule and when I asked what the next step was I was told Nicole needed to have documented proof that she was undergoing recovery counseling before she could be considered to be added to a transplant waiting list, however, in her current medical condition she was far too sick for that. I told them to arrange for a transfer back to Chattanooga so I could rebuild her strength and get her started with counseling and Nicole's 32nd birthday was just days away and I wanted her back home near family and friends.

Without skipping a beat I had scheduled Nicole at her new dialysis center and I had her first counseling appointment set for the following week but the doctor looked at me and said she was far too sick to move and only had a matter of days or weeks left. Nicole looked at me for the first time with tears in her eyes and said,

"Mom, I'm going to die aren't I?" I flew off my chair and I told her, "NO, you're not going to die. You apologize to God right now and declare that you will live and not die. No man has the right to put a time limit on your life. Jehovah Rapha is your healer and He is right here with you."

It was early Saturday morning on November 3rd and the nurse came into our room and told me to gather Nicole's belongings, they had arranged for an ambulance to transfer us back to Chattanooga and there we celebrated Nicole's 32nd birthday in a hospital room full of family and friends.

2 days later she was discharged so we could begin her new routine. Each day had its share of challenges and the hectic schedule for counseling, dialysis treatments 3 times a week and visits to the hospital for blood transfusions zapped Nicole's strength but we continued to praise God in the midst of our storm. When thoughts of fear and doubt tried to overcome us we spoke the Word.

2 Corinthians 10:5 "I cast down all negative thoughts and imaginations that try to exalt themselves above the knowledge of God and I bring into captivity every thought to the obedience of Christ Jesus."

December 2012 during a hospital stay Nicole had been bleeding from a broken vessel in the back of her nose for hours. IVs ran all day pumping her with clotting factor and blood oozed from her mouth throughout the day. As fast as I would clean her up, more blood followed. I could see that Nicole was getting weary and I tried everything to lift her spirit as I tucked her in for the night with Rapha Bear under her arm. I went home to get some rest. When I walked into her room the next morning she was sitting up with a huge smile on her face.

She said, "Mom, Jesus came to visit me last night... He leaned over my bed, wiped the blood from my lips and He wrote 'SURVIVED' on my nightgown." Looking frantically to find it and show it to me she said, "Mom, He really did come." I smiled and said, "I know He was here." And I knew that this visitation was just what Nicole needed and it gave her renewed hope and strength...

February 2013 the phone rang and it was the head doctor of the Liver Transplant Department at Vanderbilt.

He hesitantly asked, "How is Nicole doing?

I told him she was doing well and we were getting her healthy enough to bring her back and present her to the Transplant Committee. He sounded really surprised thinking by now she had passed and said that he needed to see her with his own eyes to evaluate her condition. So days later we drove her to Vanderbilt for a consultation and the doctors were amazed to see Nicole sitting on the examining table in her 'Miracles Happen' tee-shirt that she had gotten at Joan Hunters healing service in December. With a big smile on her face Nicole told the doctors,

"Yes, I am a miracle," and without hesitation they made an appointment for early April and Nicole was finally going to be considered for transplant. Our prayer had always been, "Lord, you know Nicole needs a new liver and a new kidney and we ask that your will be done either supernaturally or through transplant surgery.

The countdown had begun and in a few weeks time Nicole would finally be presented to the Liver and Kidney Transplant Committee for consideration.

It was early March 2013 and Nicole was getting one of her weekly dialysis treatments when I got a call from the nurse telling me to get to the clinic immediately. Nicole's blood pressure had plummeted and they called the ambulance to rush her to the ER. Once again the doctors said she needed to be transported back to Vanderbilt immediately. He said the time clock was ticking and something had to happen soon. Nicole's ammonia levels were off the chart; she was at risk of going into a coma from Hepatic Encepolopathy. (an occurrence of confusion, altered levels of consciousness and coma which may ultimately lead to death due to the extreme accumulation in the bloodstream of toxic substances that are normally removed by the liver.) At this stage most patients are already on the transplant waiting list and with a MELD score in the 20s. However, Nicole's MELD score had topped the charts, the highest they had ever seen which exceeded 40 and she wasn't even on the transplant list yet. She not only needed approval from the Liver Transplant Committee but she also needed approval from the Kidney Transplant Committee and neither of them met until the following week. Nicole's mind and body was under a violent attack. The enemy was doing everything in his power to once and for all try and take Nicole out. But with each and every dart he threw her way I was armed and ready with the shield of faith and the sword of the spirit; God's mighty Word.

Jehovah Rapha our Healer... "By your stripes we are healed," we were just waiting for the manifestation...

March 12, 2013 the Liver and Kidney Transplant Committees approved Nicole to be listed on March 14th at 6:00 PM. The head doctor from the Liver Transplant Team walked in our room and with a big smile on his face spoke the words I had waited to hear for 9 long months:

"Nicole has finally been approved to be listed on the United Network Organ Sharing National Registry and due to her current MELD score she will receive top priority to be matched with the first compatible donor. We will add her name in the computer tomorrow morning and it's just a matter of time for her donor to come forth."

The very next night as the nurse was doing her routine 8 PM rounds her phone rang. By the look on her face I knew something out of the ordinary was happening. She quickly made a call and scheduled Nicole to be taken down for some unexpected tests. I asked what was happening and she said as soon as she knew more she would get back to me.

My spirit jumped with joy and I knew that Nicole's donor had come forth. Here I was about to receive the greatest news of my life and the realization hit me that in order for my daughter to live someone was going to have to say good-bye to their loved one. Tears of happiness and sadness overtook me and I immediately began to pray asking the Lord to please wrap His arms of love around the donor's family and give them peace. I began thanking them for their generosity of this gift of life and for giving my daughter a second chance to reach her destiny and calling.

I could barely sleep that night due to the anticipation of the news and at 6:00 AM her doctor walked into our room and announced that all the tests had come back as needed and Nicole had a perfect donor match and she would be heading to surgery later that day to receive 2 new organs. Tears of joy rolled down my cheeks and I ran to Nicole's bedside and shared the great news with her. Unfortunately, Nicole was teetering on the edge of life and death and due to her compromised condition I don't believe she was able to comprehend the magnitude of what was about to take place. I told her God's timing was perfect and within hours her life was about to make a dramatic turn around.

Hebrews 6:15 "And so, after they had patiently endured, they obtained the promise."

Hours of pre-op preparation took place and at 8:00 PM we rolled Nicole down to surgery. With my husband by my side we said a final prayer of protection over her and at 10:30 PM Nicole's transplant surgery was underway. There was such a peace about me as I watched the clock tick away and after 7 long hours of life saving surgery at 5:30 AM, March 17th, 2013 the surgeon came with the good news that Nicole had received her new life saving liver and I could see her up in Surgical ICU but Nicole's kidney transplant had to be put on hold due to her fragile condition. As I walked in her room I was shocked by the number of pumps, IVs and the maze of wires that were connected to Nicole. There were doctors and nurses everywhere working on her continually and at 12:00 Noon they finally made the call to rush Nicole back into surgery and begin her kidney transplant. By 4:00 PM Nicole was back in SICU with her 2 new life saving organs. This was a day to be remembered forever... Nicole's new life had begun.

The worst was behind us now but there were still weeks of recovery in rehab; learning how to walk; learning how to write and learning how to adjust to her new life as a double organ transplant recipient. I was exhausted and needed some refreshing so I snuck away one Sunday morning and attended The River Church in Nashville, TN with Pastor Donny McGuire and Reba Rambo. I quietly slipped in the back of the room as Donny announced his morning sermon:

"Against All Odds" and tears of joy rolled down my cheeks when he shared the words from Job 42:2 "No plan of God's can be thwarted."

This was icing on the cake, our journey had come full circle and I cried tears of thanksgiving. God was faithful to keep His promise just as He had spoken to me through Frances Hunter back in 1991.

"Mother, fear not, my work will be accomplished."

It was just before Mother's Day and the doctors gave me the best gift ever, Nicole was finally being discharged and we could head back home to Chattanooga after living in Nashville for 3 long months. Nicole still needed round the clock care and we were kept busy running from appointment to appointment. How was the next chapter in our lives going to play out and how was Nicole going to transition back into a normal life? Only God knew but we were ready and waiting...

God was still working behind the scenes when one night a message just happened to pop up on my computer with information about New Life Bible College in Cleveland, TN that had openings for their September semester. It was just what Nicole needed and wanted as it teaches and directs individuals on how to reach their destiny and calling in ministry. Nicole immediately applied online and within 2 days she received a call from the Dean, Zona Hayes telling her she was accepted into the school and she was being gifted 2 years of college for free. It was a bit far for Nicole to travel back and forth from Chattanooga each day as she hadn't driven for over a year and again without missing a beat, God had a dorm room in a beautiful home in Cleveland available for Nicole to live in which was only minutes away from the school. Additionally, as only God could do, the Dorm Mother just happened to have previous experience taking care of a kidney transplant recipient in years past so I could rest knowing that Nicole was in good capable hands in case of an emergency. No man could have written a script that could have covered every detail of this journey with such perfection and timing. It could only be done by the hand of our loving, merciful God...

As we walked through the valley of the shadow of death, we stood on His Word and feared not. He stayed with us each and every step and comforted us through it all.

I'm sad to say that at the time of this writing the enemy is still trying to pluck Nicole from her destiny and calling but the journey isn't over and I will continue to stand on His promise...

His work will be accomplished through her… "The good work He began in her, He will bring to completion." Philippians 1:6

   I am now moving forward in this new chapter of life and ministry and I have recently launched: Starr Ministries, and I'm currently working on our first ministry outreach program: **The Rapha Bear Project** which allows me to share my testimony and message of hope with others. We share the wonderful truth of who Jehovah Rapha, our healer is and distribute Rapha Bears to those who are also in need of hope. As I step out in faith I'm believing the Lord will provide what is needed to perform this new work and I'm trusting the Lord to lead, guide and direct my path with open doors of opportunity to speak with individuals and groups to share my story: "Against All Odds." Standing in faith, walking in hope and trusting God regardless of how things look in the natural.

Psalm 105:1-2 tells us "Give praise to the Lord, proclaim His name; make known among the nations what He has done. Sing to Him, praise Him; tell all of His wonderful acts."

Contact info:

Barbara Dadswell
Chattanooga, Tennessee

E-mail: **Kingdomquotes@yahoo.com**

Visit our website: **www.StarrMinistries.net**

Facebook: Barbara Houghton Dadswell
https://www.facebook.com/ms.dadswell?fref=ts

The Rapha Bear Project on Facebook:
https://www.facebook.com/RaphaBear423/

CHAPTER 8

BARBARA WIKLUND - MADDALONI

I was healed of cancer…

When I was 28 years old and I went into the doctors for my regular check up and they discovered I had cancer of the vulva and skin cancer in my private parts; they sent me to a specialist in Albany Medical Center, to a Dr. Caputo. They confirmed the diagnosis and were going to do surgery to remove it all. When I asked the doctor how serious it was, he replied,

"You could have 6 months or none."

"I said okay," but stunned by this news. My mother was with me and I ran into the doctor's bathroom and

physically got sick. My mother asked, "May I sign the papers so my daughter can go ahead and have the surgery." And the doctor said, "No, she's got to accept it, only she can sign these papers. I tell it like it is and I tell it the worse way it could possibly be and the worse way it can be is she has no time up to 6 months to live. It's a very rare cancer."

So I came back out of the rest room and we signed the papers for surgery before leaving the doctors office. I went back home and naturally I was very upset.

My parents were upset. My father whom I was very close to used to go to this bar right over the bridge by our home, it was Junior's and he was telling the woman who runs the place about my situation. My father was so upset about this cancer scare that he shared it with this woman.

She told my dad that she was going to see Father DiOrio in Glens Falls, NY and he prayed for the sick. She urged him to give me this extra ticket to come and go with her to see Father DiOrio and hope for a healing miracle. She said to my dad,

"I have an extra ticket why don't you have her come with us."

My dad asked me to go and told me all that this woman said. I listened because I saw how upset my dad was but my first thoughts as I spoke to him were,

"I'm not going to a freak show, I've got cancer! I'm sick, I'm not going where they are yelling and screaming; I can't concentrate."

Any way my father was so upset. I could see that he was serious about this; almost desperate to help me during this time, so I agreed to go.

I said, "Okay I'll go."

One thing I forgot during this time, one day before my first surgery I found Erika my daughter who was only 8 years old outside crying, not realizing all she was over hearing. She was so scared I hugged her and told her it was going to be okay, I am sure she thought she was going to lose her mother.

During this time I want to mention that I was a real bad smoker; I smoked 5 packs of cigarettes a day from the time I got up until I went to bed at night, I constantly smoked. This is no exaggeration, I smoked 5 packs a day; a constant chain smoker; I couldn't breathe, that whole thing that goes with it, I was there.

So all the way on the ride up there to Glens Falls, NY I kept saying:

"This is a freak show; I don't want to be with these people they're old and sick."

So we go into this Glens Falls Civic Center and it was packed with people; Thousands of people; Father DiOrio was up front in this Center praying for people. I looked around and thought,

You got to be kidding me.

In the mean time Father DiOrio is bringing people up to the front praying and healing people and I was seated watching all of this. While he was praying people were dropping to the floor and doing all kinds of things and thoughts were just overwhelming my mind. I saw the large crowd of people every where and I thought,

Oh my God he's got to help that one and then another, so many sick all over. My attention kept turning to others forgetting about my own situation. Hoping all the time they would get healed.

As Father DiOrio spoke and the people that I was with told me that he was now talking about me. They said he's asking for you to come up and I was in denial saying,

"Leave me alone, no he's not!" My concern was for the others there. I kept saying to myself, 'help that one; pray for that one; help that lady; help this little girl.'

Next thing you know the Father would call out different sicknesses to every one there and I heard him say:

"There's someone here that she was being healed before she even got here; they told her she has cancer and they told her she didn't have long to live." So I'm thinking while all this is being said and the ladies I was riding with insisted that he was talking about me.

I just kept saying, "Leave me alone!" Finally the Father repeated it again and I swear to God I felt some thing go through me, it went through my whole body, some thing I've never felt before. I was like "oh boy!" And I finally went up to the front.

While realizing it was me the Father was speaking of I went up for prayer. He didn't touch me but just reiterated what he had been saying all along:

"You were being healed before you even got here. I don't know why you are fighting it but God is taking care of you. You are going to be okay, you are going to be fine. You are going to have surgery and you are going to be fine."

I told him thank you and turned around and went back to my seat.

I was lying in bed the night before the surgery and a nurse came in to take my blood pressure and get all my vitals checked ahead of time as they do. And she said to me,

"Boy, you are awful calm." I believed I was healed.

The miracle of this trip was not only did I quit smoking but I had the surgery and it was major surgery. The doctors were not sure what the outcome of the surgery would be because it was a rare cancer and they had not dealt with it much. But I knew in my heart I was healed.

I went back to the doctors for my check up and every thing was fine. So after a few months I returned to my doctors for another check up because they were keeping a close eye on me and lo and behold the cancer was back. The doctors were saying they didn't know how this was going to end because the cancer returned much too fast and I was thinking,

How could God heal me and give it back to me so quickly? Just a few months later this did not make sense to me.

Now while being at home after the second diagnosis I got angry. While at home I started throwing things because I was mad that this cancer returned and a girlfriend of mine was there and expecting me to go out that night partying. My friends at work patronized me; they were glad that I was healed but not really believing it, I could tell.

And I said, "I just got told I need surgery again and Jesus, Sue get the hell out of here. I'm not going anywhere!"

So anyway I went to bed after my friend Sue left and thinking while lying in bed that yes everyone's going to die, that's a given but I didn't believe I was going to die from the same thing He just took away from me a few months ago. I believed I was healed. So I refused to believe the depth of the diagnosis, I just didn't receive it.

"Well this is the part I want you to remember: I wasn't dreaming; God came to me just as you are sitting right here. God came to me and told me as clear as day: 'Because I didn't lose my faith I was going to be okay.'"

I went into surgery a week later or so and they could not find any cancer. After the surgery they did a scraping and recheck but the doctor said that he could not find any cancer. I returned to the doctor's office for my post-surgical check up and the doctor said as I sat there before him:

"So how come you didn't tell me?"

I said, "Tell you what?"

The doctor replied, "Well, cancer doesn't disappear; I'm a specialist and this is what I do and cancer just doesn't come and then disappear. We couldn't find any of the cancer. He continues, so there's only one answer," as he continues to search me for a response.

I replied, "What?"

He says, "Well, obviously you've had a healing. God took care of you because I didn't."

And I'll never forget this conversation. Not only did I have to go through another surgery but they could not find any cancer the second time. And I truly believe that because I didn't lose my faith, because I didn't doubt Him for taking it away the first time but because I continued to believe I was going to be okay and I was. It was as simple as that. And I am still healed today.

"I had a miracle!"

And I thought to myself why did He save me when there are so many other people that were so sick? A friend of mine answered that question when she said it was because I could then tell my story and others will be encouraged by it.

So I said, "That's it because there were so many others suffering so much more. But I believe when I was in that meeting and I was so concerned about the others well-being that I got healed. I wasn't concerned for myself at all; I was already being healed at that time."

"I saw Jesus face to face and it's the truth too, when I had cancer the second time I had a visitation."

The second time the cancer came back I knew that God had already healed me the first time. I did not believe He put it on me again. I didn't believe that God would heal you of something only to give it right back to you a few months later. That would be a slap in the face!

One more thing after my surgery I was staying at my mother's home and I was lying on the couch and my brother came in and put a pillow and blanket on the floor next to me, I said what are you doing and he said that I am just going to sleep here next to you in case you need something, it was as meaningful as if God was speaking to me because he cared so much. Who would have guessed my story would end up in a book for people to read and that you would be the one to make it happen? God had a plan from the beginning!

Again I want to say that I wondered why I was chosen to be healed and my friend Fran said it was to tell my story and I tell it all the time to anyone who needs to hear it. I don't care who believes me, I continue to tell others about my healing. I don't care if you think I'm crazy or if you think I imagined it; I would've died by now. This is 37 years ago this happened and I am still here telling about it today. I wasn't scared but it really happened, I can still see it all in my mind and actually the way God spoke it to me. I can recall it each and every time. I was awake and I knew it was God and I knew I was going to be okay. Was it a test, I truly don't know but I knew I went through it and I continued to return to see the specialist up to maybe two years ago and the cancer has never returned. I had to have a hysterectomy but nothing to do with that former condition. Like I said before we're all going to die, we're not going to be on this earth forever but I am not going to die of that particular condition I had so many years ago which was a rare cancer. I'm still telling the story today and whether you believe me or not I'm going to continue to tell it.

John & I visited Schenectady, NY where Barb lives. She told us this story as we recorded it on our video camera to retype later in her beautiful backyard garden as we visited that wonderful day; Monday, June 26th, 2016 around noon time. The sun was shining and Barb & I were smiling because we hadn't seen each other for many years as I had moved away from my birth place city. Barb & I went to school together and as we visited her story of healing which was revealed to us that day; A story of God's love for His children. We're so thankful to Barb for sharing her miracle with us and now with you the readers of this book. We hope you can see and believe in the healing power of our Lord Jesus Christ.

Contact info:

Barbara Wiklund - Maddaloni
Schenectady, New York

E-mail: **bmaddaloni@hotmail.com**

Facebook: Barbara Wiklund-Maddaloni

https://www.facebook.com/barbara.wiklundmaddaloni?fref=ts

CHAPTER 9

MAGGIE BROCK

My home was a loving peaceful place...

My story starts out from a child I was raised in a very strict religious Christian home. I was the youngest of 14 and we children were very loved and cared for even though my parents struggled financially. My Father and Mother were both traveling ministers of the gospel and we would move around a lot sometimes sleeping in our vehicles and once I remember waking up under the vehicle where some of my siblings and I had slept that night. But again I was very loved by my parents, never abused or neglected. They took care of me the best they could. My Father and Mother rarely argued and when they would the only way that we would know that they were fighting is that my dad would step out into his vehicle for a time and my mom would clean the house vigorously. Then after awhile of that they would come back together as if nothing had happened.

Now I'm sure they had words and discussed things but we as kids never would hear it. My home was a loving peaceful place, I grew up in this atmosphere; the atmosphere where a man respected women, never hitting her, never using harsh words. My dad displayed a loving example of how a husband should treat his wife, so when I got married my expectation was to be loved and treated this same way.

I was 20 years old when I married my husband after just two months of meeting him for the first time. Our story began when my best friend moved from Florida where I lived, to Kentucky with her family and her father being my former pastor whom I respected highly.

We kept in touch by phone and by mail. Now I had been ministering at some small churches in my area and also was asked to minister at some youth revivals and was just starting to step out in what I had known from a child that which I was called to do. At this time they started to pastor a church and invited me up to visit and to help out as we talked more about me visiting, they also talked about this young man they wanted me to meet. This young man attended their church and was my age and they thought very highly of him. They had also spoken to him about me and he was interested, in fact so interested that he started writing me by mail. Well it wasn't long until he shared his intention to marry me, in fact it was in the second letter that I received from him that he said that God had shown him that he was suppose to marry me, but I thought that he was crazy for suggesting this because we hadn't met yet. With all of this going on I made arrangements to go visit my Pastor friends for a month, staying with them. The very day that I arrived the guy that they spoke so highly of came to visit me; we were introduced and I had no interest at all, but my former pastor whom I had gotten saved under and respected very highly and seen as a father figure told me that he thought that he was the one for me that I should marry him. You have to understand I was very young at the time and the religion that I had grown up in taught that whatever the pastor or man of God said was so, that settled it; there was no room for questioning. So after a month I went back to Florida and he came and moved in my sister's home until we got married a month later.

My marriage seemed to be going good and everything was normal until the third month when we moved into a small trailer that we rented from one of my dad's friends. Somewhere in the beginning of my marriage I fell madly in love with this guy (my husband) that I had not liked when we first met, and I was looking forward to living out the picture that I had of a wonderful, loving, happy marriage! Somewhere in the fourth month of our marriage he started to show signs of depression, anger and so we began to fight a lot. He said it was because he missed his family and wanted to move us back to live in Kentucky near his mom and dad, but I was pregnant. So I begged him to wait until after I gave birth. So three months after I had given birth to my first child he moved us to Kentucky to live with his parents, until we found a place. And this is when the abuse started; it started out verbal, then he began throwing things in anger or pouring drinks on me or taking my baby away from me and having his mother lock herself and my child up in a room and wouldn't let me see her until I agreed to do or act the way he thought I should. You see nothing was ever his fault, it was always mine, I was the trouble maker, I made him do it, and I was always doing wrong.

You might say, "Why did his family let him do this to me?" Because what I didn't know at the time was that this was how he was raised and he wasn't raised like I was in a loving home with awesome parents no, his parents were very controlling and abusive to him.

Shortly after we found a place to rent and moved into it not far from his parents house, I got pregnant with my second child. The anger and the verbal abuse continued and had gotten worse and the physical was beginning to start even more but he would only hit in places on me that were hidden so no other could see, like he would pound on the back of my head with his fist or he would hit my back, upper arm, thigh area, he would still throw things at me like food and drinks. I prayed for the protection of my unborn baby and God kept her safe and my oldest was only fifteen months old when I had my second child and he didn't care if she saw what he did to me or not.

I began to see that my husband acted like two different people at times and I just couldn't understand how he could be loving and happy one minute and the next second be angry and treat me so horribly, but then again I did not know about all that he went through as a child and even up into his adulthood until he left to get married, as I look back I think marrying me was a way that he thought would get him free from the abuse and the pain that he had suffered. But when you don't get healed from the past pain you will return to it in some way or another.

You may ask, "Ok so why didn't you leave him?" I tried many times but my love for him and my religious beliefs that God hated divorce kept me with him.

So I began to pray that God would change him and would heal my marriage. The abuse had gotten worse, real bad in fact. He would move us every three to six months from town to town, church to church so no one would find out that this wonderful preacher (my hubby) was very abusive to his family. He isolated me from family and friends, I wasn't allowed to have friends or if my co-workers asked me to go out, I wasn't allowed to go. He never physically abused my girls but in his anger he would corner them and intimidate them, and verbally abuse them, he isolated himself from them. He just didn't know how to love like a father should. Somewhere around our 7th year of marriage he started to have affairs with other women, meeting them in hotel rooms. At this time he became addicted to pornography and meeting women in chat rooms. He was also drawn to the occult, satanism, the brotherhood and also wiccans. Now he said that he was witnessing to them but he would attend their meetings and have close relationships with them having personal phone calls with them. As I had said before he was like two different people; he would try his best to be good and kind and to try and not look at porn or stopping the occult things but he said that I was a horrible wife and that I drove him to cheat. I lived everyday with his words of being told I was an awful wife and that he never loved me and it was my fault that he acted the way he did and after so long of being told these things it just becomes part of you, you start to believe it. Everything that once was me wasn't there anymore, I was broken…

I had stopped ministering because it was all about him and his ministry. I had become depressed, withdrawn and I cowered at his voice and around the 12th year of our marriage, I stopped praying,

"God heal my marriage, God make this stop to praying, God I can't take this any longer, save me please."

Around the 15th year of my marriage I finally told my husband if this doesn't change then I'm leaving because I can't handle it any more. He of course did not believe me because he was happy, comfortable the way things were. But for me the years of having to hide out in the bathrooms with my girls, or lock ourselves up in the bedroom putting dressers up against the door, locking ourselves up in our vehicle until the morning so he couldn't get to us because his temper flared up…

All the years of putting on the smiles and pretending we were the perfect little Christian family while at church or in front of others. And then on the way home being beat in the head because he wasn't being treated at church the way he thought that he should have been. All the years of not being able to hold down a job because my husband needed me at home with him always; all the years of having ice-cream, drinks and food in general thrown at me; all the years of seeing my children live in this verbal abuse and neglected by their father; all the years of being cheated on and feeling worthless, and rejected; all these years of neglect and abuse had left me hurt, and rejected; I was broken.

My rescue came shortly after 15 years of marriage. My husband decided to move us to Tennessee so he could attend New Life Bible College to get his degree. At least that was his intentions but God had actually heard my cry and he brought us here to rescue me, to heal my marriage and to heal my family. Within the first year we were there God showed my pastor that my family needed healing and that there was something wrong with my family situation. So she called my husband one day and told him what God had shown her and asked if she could speak with us so she could counsel us and get us help. Of course he got scared because everything that he worked so hard to keep secret was being exposed and he would have to deal with his own inner hurts, so he ran literally. He had me drive him to the Greyhound bus station and he got on it and left. He called my pastor a week later and told her that he didn't want anything else to do with me and the girls. Of course he called me several times a day to ask me to move back to Kentucky with him and there was a part within me that loved him and a part that grew accustomed to that way of life and wanted to say yes. But the pain and the brokenness cried out no, I was done I needed to be rescued. So we agreed to a separation or should I say I wanted the separation of course he didn't. But I told him unless things changed I wasn't going back into that lifestyle again. But he didn't feel that he needed to change.

He retaliated by giving my number to ministers that didn't know our situation and he would have them call me and tell me that it's a sin for me to leave and divorce my husband and that I needed to learn to submit, he was very vicious in telling lies about me to whoever would listen. He made my life a living nightmare even though I was away from him he continued the verbal abuse. He tried to get my kids taken away from me and put them in a home. His way of thinking was if I can't have them you can't either. He stalked me and threatened me. He even hired a witch to put a love spell on me and to curse my pastor.

My life at this time was such a mess, my marriage was broken, my heart was broken, my emotions were broken, my girls were broken, my life and everything that I knew from the age of 20 was gone pretty much and now at the age of 39 I was going to start over. But God had plans to heal me and he heard my cries and He rescued me and my girls. Then I yielded and God started taking me through the healing process. He put me in a place where my girls and I would be accepted and loved and cared for. He knew exactly what He was doing when he led my ex to bring us to New Life, His perfect plan was to bring us here to heal my family but it takes two people in a marriage for a change to happen. I will tell you that the healing process was not easy, but what made it bearable is the church family that God had given me. My pastor told me that she wanted my girls and me to attend her Bible College, the same one my ex started so that we could be under the healing power of the Word. So we did and it was the best thing that I could have ever done. It was the first steps in God's plan for me. After about two years of separation my husband filed for divorce and three months later it was legal and he became my ex. He not only divorced me but since he divorced our girls, his daughters too. He cut off all ties with them except every now and then he'd pop back into their lives with a letter stating how wonderful his life was and that he didn't want them in his new life. Do I think he ever loved his daughters, yes, I do but in his own way all wrapped up in the hurts from his past. In the healing process I learned to forgive, to forgive the verbal and physical abuse, I had to forgive him for all the years that he took from me; I had to forgive him for abandoning our children. I had to walk in forgiveness daily.

You have heard my testimony of how the devil tried to stop me and to eventually destroy me but now let me tell you my redemption story, because you see the person that you have just read about with all the brokenness, hurts, abandonment issues, rejection issues, self hatred, feelings of worthlessness is no longer here! All of that is no longer a part of my life God heard my cry and rescued me and healed me and gave me a new life. He gave me a life that is filled with love, peace, joy, laughter and a happy life. I'm surrounded by family and friends, I'm excited about life. I have attended the same church for 5 years now and they have placed me in several leadership positions and I am over the Victorious Women's Ministry at the church which is growing and thriving.

  I have just graduated with a 4 year Bachelors Degree in Christian Ministry from New Life Bible College, where I currently teach students from all walks of life. My girls are in my life and have grown to be mighty women of God. My oldest daughter is married giving me my first grandchild and my youngest daughter leading worship in the church we all attend together and will be going to The Ramp School of Worship in Hamilton, Alabama to further her career as a worship leader. All those 18 years of marriage God rescued me when I cried out to Him and now He is ordering my steps to get us right where we needed to be and that's what God did for me, He rescued me!

Zephaniah.3:17 For the Lord your God is living among you. He is a mighty savior. He will take delight in you with gladness. With his love, he will calm all your fears. He will rejoice over you with joyful songs."

Contact info:

Maggie Brock
Cleveland, Tennessee

E-mail: **maggiebrock212@yahoo.com**

Facebook: Maggie Brock

https://www.facebook.com/maggie.brock.526

CHAPTER 10

WENDY WHITE

Broken and bent ready for the Master's use…

   I am healed and I want my story to be used to bring healing to others. That is after all the greatest blow that we can throw at the enemy, taking what he did and using it as a weapon against him.

   While I am able to do that, I have come to realize that many aren't at that place in their healing. Time doesn't heal all things, only Jesus does that. The problem is that we have to let Him into those places and allow Him to heal them. We keep things bottled up, like they were treasures, under lock-in-key. We even have a no trespassing sign up that Jesus isn't allowed passed it.

To truly allow Him to heal us, we have to unlock every door, pull down every sign, and be willing to deal with all the pain and ugliness of our lives. It is only through all of this that we will receive our freedom. So many of those that I love are still bound up because they can't withstand the pain to get to their healing; I've witnessed this first-hand and dealt with the painful lashes that I received as a consequence. It takes wisdom and compassion in dealing with others brokenness and I'm sorry to say I've lacked both most of my life.

For the most part, this may come across as random thoughts pieced together and it is; I just have random memories rolling around in my head and I want this to be as authentically me as it possibly can be.

I hope you fight through my tragedy and find your way to my triumph.

As you read this memory I want you to keep in mind that I tell this with the memory and feelings of a child, not an adult. We experience things as children and most adults expect us to process them as adults. I am going to convey to you what I experienced and felt in the moment, not what I feel or think today. I have since come to see things in a different light. I love my mother very much. God has restored our relationship in many ways and I honor the woman of God that she is.

When I was eight years old my mother packed up the family SUV, loaded us kids up and took us to Grandma's. From there we went to church camp. My uncle was there with one of his wives, I don't recall her name at this time. We were in a room, I don't remember what the room looked like, and I only remember my mother having a big spider smashed in a Kleenex inside of her purse. She got it out and said,

"There was a spider just like this at church camp when I was a kid."

The next memory I have is that she was gone and we were at my uncle's house. My daddy was trying to get us kids back, the police were involved and we went home with daddy.

My mind can't piece together the time frame of events at this point.

Daddy took us to the hospital to see mother and she had left. Daddy told us she left because she didn't want to see us. Later we went to another hospital and she was there. We went in to see our mother, the woman we found looked like our mother, but she didn't act like our mother. She didn't even know who I was. Some weeks later she got to come home, but she was never really my mother again.

She stayed for a few more years and then she divorced my father. She didn't tell us kids anything about why she was leaving but our father told us plenty. He said she left because she wanted to be with men instead of us. I believed him because he was my daddy. Why would he lie to me? It wasn't until I was a teenager that my mother explained to me why she had left. You take a person who comes from a family who has worked very hard but has had very little and you put them with someone whose family has worked very hard but has had plenty and gave him all that he ever wanted and there is bound to be some very different mindsets. She would save to pay bills and he would take the money and go buy a horse and then go asked his parents for the money to pay the bills. She couldn't live like this; it wasn't the way she was raised. I never remember them fight and mother would say they didn't because she wanted to be a good wife and just do whatever daddy wanted.

There is a price to pay for freedom and it may end up being more expensive than you anticipate.

We were told to do whatever we wanted to in order to drive mother crazy so that she would quit fighting for us. She only wanted our check, in which he was taking care of a man with. Many years later I realized it was my daddy who couldn't stand that mother got our social security checks. It takes money to feed and clothe three kids.

We put our mother through hell. That's the nicest description I have for what we did. She was literally tortured by her own kids for about four years. That's on top of being drug in and out of court for every little thing you can imagine. Every cut, scrape, or bruise turned into another visit to court.

I began developing earlier than most girls which caused a lot of self consciousness. My Papaw couldn't keep his hands to himself and would pinch me on my breast every time I walked by him. One day Mamaw stood up to him and told him to keep his hands off of me and he never did it again. That didn't stop him from peeking through my bathroom window though.

Looking back we had been such sheltered children and at the point of the divorce it was as if the gates of hell had been swung wide open on us. One night when I was 10 or 11 dad took us in the middle of the night and sat on the street in front of a house. He told us that our mother was in that house having sex and he went into much more detail. Then he took us to a large popular retail store's parking lot and told us that we were free to call our mother anything that we wanted to. Now mind you at this point I didn't have the first clue about sex and this was the first time sex had ever been discussed around me.

I went to church camp for the first time in my life with a large denominational church kids and I had such a good time. I met some wonderful people there. I think what I liked most was the fact that I was away from all of the drama in my life.

Where I went to school, when you began the fifth grade you had to change your clothes for P.E. A few times I came home and I didn't have my top button buttoned on my shirt and I got sat down at the kitchen table and my Dad and Mamaw explained to me how I was acting like a slut and a whore, just like my Momma.

I never felt like my Daddy loved me. I always thought since I looked more like my Mom, he saw her when he looked at me and that was why. I knew he loved my brother and sister, it was evident. For a long time I tried to gain his approval. He never once told me I did a good job, I could have always done better. When I was in my teens my mother once told me that daddy never wanted me and that he cried when I was born because I was a girl. My sister was obviously a girl too but he didn't cry about her.

Its funny looking back and thinking about what others thought of me and my life and everything they thought he did for us. The truth is most of what they thought he did for us was him doing for himself. We just got to go along for the ride.

Well, you've made it this far and it's about to get interesting. You may never be able to look at me the same way again. I'm about to let you in on some of my own darkest secrets, and yet there are even darker secrets that I placed in the hands of Jesus, where they are safely covered in the blood. They are forgiven. They are of no benefit to you or to me and therefore I leave them there. I only tell you about them being there so that you can know that it is okay to leave some of yours there too. God once told me that the devil is in the details and that is so true. We are saved by the blood of the lamb and the word of our testimony. Our testimony is about the goodness of Jesus and His delivering power in our lives. Some details need to be shared so that others know what you lived through. The fact that I'm still alive after every attempt that the devil made to take me out is the encouragement that someone needs today to get back up and keep fighting. Therefore I gladly give you my details. My freedom story is the key that will unlock many of God's daughters in this hour. Your freedom is worth the price I'll pay with all of my transparency.

I was fourteen, setting in my grandma's church and I remember the Holy Spirit tugging at my heart for the first time in my life. I made my way down to the altar, where the pastor and others gathered around me. They were more concerned with the earrings in my ears than they were with my soul. They asked me to remove my earrings. I was so confused. I went from experiencing the Holy Spirit's conviction to human condemnation in 0.2 seconds flat.

I didn't go back and it wasn't long after that, that we all quit going to church period. We did have lots of horse riding to do on Sunday afternoon after all. Dad took us out one night and got us drunk on a popular whiskey and mixed with colas from our local drive in. I guess in his mind he was going to show us how bad it was so that we wouldn't want to do it any more. I got drunk. Fought the vacuum in the backseat because I had puked all down the side of the door and I got to clean it all up the next day. Needless to say, Dad's attempt to turn me away from drinking did not work.

It was around this time that I got my horse Cody. Dad and I drover over to Missouri to look at her, she was the most beautiful horse I had ever seen. Solid black and built like a quarter horse should be, with square hips. She was perfect. I wanted her but the price they were asking was twice as much as any other horse we had ever owned. We went home and dad told Mamaw about her and I begged for her, like I'd never begged for anything, and Mamaw gave in and she was mine. Riding her was the greatest rush of my life. She was so fast and you never really knew if you would be able to stop her. She was also my best friend. I would tell her my secrets and my heartaches. I felt like a horse loved me more than any of the people in my life. She would be the thing that was held over my head in days to come. If I left and went to live with mother they would sell her. When I went to stay with mother, if I didn't come back they would sell her.

As a freshman in high school I began to sneak out of the house. The first time I snuck out of Mamaw and Papaw's I took Papaw's liquor and mixed it with sweet tea. BAD IDEA! The person who talked me into this would years later be the very first person to talk me out of it. Most people just want you to make them look better and the only way they can do that is by pulling you down to their level. They get you into the ditch with them and they will use you as their step ladder to get out.

The next time I snuck out I gave away my virginity. The sad thing is I gave myself to someone I didn't care anything about. I was just doing it to be doing it. Then I told my mother about it just to break her heart. This was just the beginning of my life spiraling out of control. The next few months I had sex with a few other boys. Then, by the time I was fifteen, I was completely out of control. I snuck out nearly every night that year. I didn't care who picked me up as long as they got me drunk or high, I would give myself to them.

They nailed every window in the house shut except for the bathroom window. They didn't think I could get in and out of it, since it was so high off of the ground. I had such a demonic hold on me that nothing was going to keep me in that house. I would leave after Dad went to sleep and come back in take a shower and leave for school.

I know that if it wasn't for the grace of God I would be dead.

Once I had snuck out and gone to the river, where there was a party in progress. I got drunk and ended up in the river with a man I didn't know. He held my head under the water about three times. He was trying to kill me. I got away and found my way back to the person I came with.

I tried several times to kill myself. The first time I took a mixture of my Dad's pills and passed out on the living room floor. The pills disappeared after that. The next time I took an entire bottle of menstrual medication. I tried to cut my wrist but as painful as it was the razor blade just wouldn't cut my skin. I had left my suicide note on the back of my bedroom door in lipstick. It didn't come off it just smeared. The last time I took an entire pack of diet pills; I decided real fast that that wasn't the way I wanted to die. My head felt as if it was in a vice and it was squeezing shut on me. I called my mother and she took me to the emergency room. It took awhile for the pain to go away.

Years later, after I was born again, a girl from school said that I scared her every day by telling her I was going home to kill myself. She was a Christian. She prayed for me. Her prayers are probably a big reason why I'm still here today.

Somewhere in the midst of all of this my mother had another episode. Her boyfriend came and checked me out of school and took me to the doctor's office that she was at. I went back to see her and she had my scrapbook with her. She told me that she was going to be my fairy god mother. She had found a private detective that was going to marry me. Then she said I know you have slept with one person, how many more? I left the room crying. Grandma was in the waiting room and she took me back to school.

I didn't know it then, but from that day forward I took all the blame on myself for her sickness. Even into my adulthood I wouldn't speak truth to her out of fear that I would push her over the edge, at least not in normal conversation. There were plenty of times that I blew up and let her have it.

I spent the night with a friend and went to the lake and got drunk one Sunday. Momma came to get me and I wasn't going to leave. I talked horribly to her and called her most everything I could think of but she wouldn't leave me. Years later she told me that she knew if she left me there that day she would have lost me forever. So, she stood here and took everything I threw at her and then she took me home.

My first car was a foreign make which I totaled not long after I got my driver's license. We all headed to Chickasaw and daddy had told me to meet him at a store on the way. I had run around doing some things I wasn't supposed to do and so I was a little late and went on. Not far down the road

I decided I probably needed to go back to that store. At the next red light I turned out in front of a van that I never saw coming.

The next thing I remember is my friend screaming she's dead, she's dead and then a man praying over me. I was taken to the hospital in an ambulance. The only thing wrong with me was a pulled muscle in my back. The state trooper told my dad that he wouldn't give me a ticket for not having a seatbelt on because if I had had it on it would have snapped my neck. I know this was my fault but looking back I never remember daddy ever showing concern for my health at any time that I got hurt. He would always fuss at me for what I had done. I was always afraid of seeing him because I knew I would be in trouble. The sad thing is I carried all of that over to my children. There should be punishment for the things that we do wrong but it should never supersede our love. I think this is why it has taken me so long to truly understand and accept the love that the Father has for me. In those moments that I feel like I don't deserve anything from His hand, that's when He blesses me the most.

It was January 1990; I was 16 when I began dating Jamie. I had seen him around, been in many of the same places, but he had never been interested. He was just different. He had a heart that was tender underneath the adolescent drug use. So we began dating which was mostly getting high and having sex. But, he actually cared about me and I couldn't imagine why. I didn't feel as if I deserved to be cared about the way that he cared about me.

After we were married and had our oldest son, I began to go to church again. This time it was very different. It was a different denomination, there wasn't any condemnation but there wasn't any conviction either. I was going because I thought it was the right thing to do and wanted my kids to be in church. My Mamaw died around this time. She and I had had a falling out which really weighed heavily on my heart. I got baptized while I was pregnant. Even though I went regularly nothing about me changed, I was still the same person, with the same sailor's mouth and attitude that I had always had. After I had our youngest son I got my tubes tied and therefore had no fear of becoming pregnant again and soon I began to get high again.

During the next several years I would probably be a walking definition of crazy. I did and said most of what popped into my head. I spent the next 8 years in many ups and downs; Valleys of depression and drug addiction. The thing that weighs heaviest on my heart is the way that I treated my kids. I battled with rage and anger most of my life. It was a generational familiar spirit.

When I was 30 years old I bought myself the famous book series about the rapture for Christmas. Up to this point I think I had read only a handful of books. Reading wasn't one of my favorite things to do. I picked up the first one and couldn't quit. I had the whole series read in two weeks. Reading these books made me question what the Bible really said. I picked up the Bible and began to read it. For the first time I really understood what it was saying. I realized that I had led my family into hell and it was up to me to pull them out.

My kids had begun going to church up the road earlier that year and would constantly ask me and Jamie to come with them. We were full of excuses. Conviction had set in my heart though. Since the kids were already going there I decided that I would just go with them. I made a public confession of my faith that day. A few months later I was baptized. I was delivered from cigarettes the night before I was baptized. I have never wanted one since.

There was an evangelist who came a few weeks after I got saved. I was setting in the back and the Lord told me to go down for prayer. I said to the Lord I'll go but I'm not going to fall to the floor and act all crazy like those people. I went down and when he came to pray for me, he barely touched my head and down I went. I had no control. I saw in my mind a giant roman pillar falling in slow motion. I lay there for awhile unable to move. When I got up I was filled with a boldness that I had never known before. I went home and called everyone that I could think of and told them that they needed to come to revival. I even called my daddy and told him that if he came he would be healed. That was the level of faith and boldness that came upon me that night. Daddy didn't come, but that didn't change my mind about the power of God.

I would go to revival seeking the Holy Ghost with the evidence of speaking in tongues and when it finally happened I was at home kneeling beside my bed. I believe I was filled the night I received the boldness, but I just didn't know how to release what was on the inside of me. I think far too often we have to battle our thoughts and preconceived notions before we can step into what the Holy Spirit has for us.

I shared what had happened with my Momma and she invited me to a prayer meeting. I wasn't going to go because I was still in between but heard the Holy Spirit begin to scream,

"GET UP! GET UP! GET UP!'

I called Momma back and told her I would be there. It was one of the greatest decisions of my life. I have attended this prayer meeting ever since. I only missed one year because I didn't get a lunch at my job and this prayer meeting took place at this time. This same prayer meeting has been going on for 51 years and the precious Mother over it is right at 94 years of age. I have been blessed to get to witness her faithfulness. This prayer meeting has been the key to my journey with Christ. They have taught me how to pray. They have prayed for me. They have encouraged me and believed in me. They have walked me through some of the most difficult times in my life. God knew that I would need prayer warriors in my life that knew how to pray.

It's hard to explain to someone what being born again is. All I know is that I was no longer the same person. I could understand the Word of God and I consumed it. You hear all of these clichés about everything going good for you after you get saved and how being part of the church is like having a family. Well my life is good and I praise God for it and I love the church but these sayings are just that, sayings. I have had to fight my battle. I've had good days and I have had lots of days that I have had to cover in the blood. I have found people in the body who have become family to me but as far as the church I attended becoming my family, which has never been my experience. I tried many years to fit in and do all the things that good Christians should do in the church, all the while just becoming miserable. When you have more on the inside of you, you will never be satisfied just having religious rituals for church. Holy Spirit gnawed away inside of me for the more and I had to push Him down because I didn't know what to do with Him. I felt like such an oddball, like I didn't fit it. I knew from the time I was filled with His Spirit that he didn't call me to set on a pew and become like everyone else but most people don't want what I carry.

I am too much for most people. I hear God's voice plainly and He gives me exact instructions at times. Most people in the church don't know what it is to hear the voice of God and they reject even the thought. This is not Biblical. We try to put everything into a pretty little box and make everything stay within the lines. We can't do that because our God is bigger than any box we can draw out and any line we can measure.

Church was a struggle for me. I met many wonderful loving people. I learned so much in Sunday school and I was growing but the fairy tale of everyone else's experience was not my experience. I was carrying around a spirit of rejection and instead of being delivered from it, it was being fed. So many days I left Church crying begging God to let me leave that Church. Everything that the enemy had always said to me about being unlovable he now had strong ammunition to shoot at me. See even your Pastor hates you. I truly didn't know what was wrong with me. I only wanted to obey the Lord. People would preach and teach and they would devote their messages to me. Not out of some word from the Holy Spirit but from personal knowledge about me and situations in my life. It was like daggers being thrown from all directions when I went to church. The very people that everyone thought so much of because they were "such good Christians" were the very people that I personally experienced the vilest evil come out of. We are killing people, their hopes and dreams, their uniqueness every day by shoving them into our man made boxes. Jesus saves us and we are these great rays of light and then we walk into our denominations and they hand us a set of clothes so we can look like them. Those clothes are designed to cover up the light. We are supposed to look like Jesus not our denomination. I believe in this hour God is raising up people who are going to refuse to wear the clothes that man is handing them. These burning ones are going to let their light shine like no other generation. The only clothes they will need is the righteousness of Jesus.

Some things you don't even know how to begin. These last few years have definitely been a wild ride to say the least.

   I walked through a season of utter misery. I was sick of going to church. The church wasn't feeding me. I was getting much more out of my personal Bible study. There was no life in the message from the pulpit, only condemnation, and let's all hold on another day till Jesus comes back for us. I became bitter and critical of everything. The Lord began to deal with me. He had me quit my job and then he began to show me myself little by little. I don't think I would have been able to bear it all at once.

   God began to stir me to pray for revival. In 2015 the first thing God told me to do was to drive around my county praying. It took four hours to get around the edge of the county. People went with me each time and we made seven or eight trips, different people and different routes each time. I didn't know what I was doing at the time other than being obedient. The fall of that year was the first time I heard my Apostle; he caused something to leap on the inside of me. For the first time I heard someone speak the very things that God had been speaking to me.

   This was a new season of strange obedience for me. The Lord began sending me to places to meet people that I really didn't know outside of our social media. Before all of this I had never been further than an hour away from my house alone and I never had a desire to travel. I wasn't as bad as Jamie, the fifteen minute drive to town use to be more than he wanted to endure.

After awhile I realized what God was trying to show me. It was okay to just do this the way He was laying it out. All of these places were a very unique expression. They each flowed in their own grace. They were not carbon copies. They weren't structured programs. They each flowed with the Spirit in the way that the Spirit wanted to flow uniquely through them. Even though I was doing all these things and going all these places I was still battling rejection. It felt like I was going ten rounds a day with this stinking spirit and twenty on the way home from conferences.

It was a real struggle trying to figure out my role in going to Church. At first I tried to go back into it and do all the same old things but God made it abundantly clear that He didn't want that for me. He had to tell me over and over again that I was only there to stand in the gap for them. I was not to be influenced by them in any shape or form. This made the battle even worse. I had to put so many things to death in me during this season.

This whole journey has been a wild ride. At the end of 2016 the Lord had told me that this year was going to be like a whirlwind and right after that I saw two huge whirlwinds right in the road in front of me, which had never happened before. I can tell you that this year has been like a whirlwind.

God has sent me out and stretched me in every direction. I have heard people talk and I know that they think I am chasing after something. They would be wrong and right at the same time. The thing they think I'm chasing isn't what I'm chasing. You see, I'm chasing after God and where He has been leading me is to the unlocking of Wendy. I know that sounds strange to you but in every step of this crazy journey God has had me on I've gotten a little freer every time I've obeyed. I've become revival. He has become my closest companion. The more in me has been awakened and even in the small state of its beginnings it rose up and slayed the giants in the land of Wendy. The more uncovered everything hidden by deception and caused me to look at myself straight in the face. One at a time the giants were killed; the giant of rage, self-righteousness, pride, fear and rejection. They have no power over the more in you. The more in you is Jesus and He is just waiting on you to die so that you can freely live.

If there is a celebration in heaven over every lost sinner saved I can't imagine the celebration that is going on in heaven when we take our first step into our destiny. Can't you just hear Jesus saying,

"Yes finally."

We are sons and daughters of destiny but we are fighting against all of hell for that destiny. God constantly wants to unlock the next in us. We never arrive as long as we are flesh and blood.

Luke 7:47 "I tell you, her sins--and they are many--have been forgiven, so she has shown me much love. But a person who is forgiven little shows only little love."

* Wendy White has recently authored her own book titled: **My Undoing by Wendy White**. Now available on Amazon.com

Contact info:

Wendy White
Finley, Tennessee

E-mail: **w4family@yahoo.com**

Facebook: **https://www.facebook.com/wendynjamiew**

CHAPTER 11

NANCY HERROLD

I am in the palm of His hand...

At age 22, I married a young man who had a great vision for his future in the field of medicine. I was not saved and as the topic was not discussed while dating, or in marriage. I assume looking back, he was unsaved as well. Nine years into the marriage, we decided to begin our family as we had our foundation ready to build upon (our financial foundation). Shortly after the baby was born, my husband left us for another woman. His request was we leave the state and he would provide the finances for a moving truck; he asked for reasonable visitation only...

We were becoming debt free, looking to buy a home, car, etc. I had no clue this was on the horizon. Even though I thought I was courageous, traveling with my husband in the pursuit of his career goals, working sometimes three jobs to sustain us, excited to enlarge our family while returning to school myself, I was gripped by intense fear! Worry enveloped me; what if someone breaks into our home, kills me, and leaves the baby crying? How long could it be before someone would check on us and find the child? How was I going to secure full time employment and raise a child myself?

How would I find safe living arrangements in another state, and which state? Also, the baby cried all the time as there was usually respiratory distress. (I didn't realize until we were moving out of our house that it was filled with mold from the crawl space through the attic.) Yes, I missed my husband's companionship; however, I thought he would change his mind and return home. (This did not occur.) In the interim, fear paralyzed me as I didn't know how to make a solid decision for myself and a child. I had very, very little experience with children and what I knew up to this point came from books/reading material.

My cousin-in-law sent me by mail a tract sharing Jesus. I was in my room studying it. It made no sense to me. Although my mind conceived there was a higher power than man, it went no farther than this. From childhood until this point in life, I hadn't even attended church and didn't understand why others did. There were always more productive things to do with time, I reasoned. In reciting the tract, I invited Jesus to be my Lord and Savior… Please understand, I had NO idea what that meant. Immediately, there was a peace that came over me. I can still remember the evening as if it were a few moments ago. The fear was abated and I heard a soothing voice say,

"It's going to be alright."

I thought it was a unique way of talking to myself; however I embraced these words.

(It was the HOLY SPIRIT.)

Oh, it took almost a year before I realized this truth. That night, I slept through as well as my baby; we slept through the entire night!!! The next day, and for the next several months He was guiding me without my knowledge. I thought I was getting these creative ideas of how to find a safe home out-of-state, child care, employment, etc. (Even though my ex-husband did provide support, it was not enough to care for us without supplemental income.) I called a realtor from out of state, and was connected with a knowledgeable, service oriented one. We conducted business by snail mail at the time. There was a desire in me to read the Bible. (There was one in the house, interestingly enough.) I opened the pages and landed upon Noah and the Ark. Well, this was beyond my comprehension thinking this book must be analogies that need to be explained by a church leader. I drove to the nearest church building with my child to check it out. My child went to childcare and I attended service. It was so boring. I could not understand how anyone could tolerate this. Must be they teach discipline and faithfulness such as military training. If this is how life is, I will come; however, I will stay in the childcare room and watch the kids interacting! I learned nothing about this entity, Jesus.

Finally, the realtor called and it was time to move. The realtor directed me to his office in Florida and took me and my child to our home. The moving truck came shortly afterwards. We spent the first few nights in a hotel, as paperwork needed to be finalized and utilities turned on. I knew nobody in this town…

First night in the house, still before the furniture arrived, we slept on the floor. My child was unable to sleep and I discovered that the house was ant infested. They were biting all night… Before dawn, we got out of the house and walked in the neighborhood (stroller in tow) to see if anyone was awake yet. First household we came upon became our great friends. In the first few months of residency, we made incredible friendships and alliances in our neighborhood. We became family, everybody fellowshipping and helping one another. One neighbor suggested a church. We attended and I began learning who Jesus is. He is God. My heart wanted more of Him and He directed our steps.

My child at under the age of three began speaking to the Holy Spirit, learning about Him and His ways at church as well. Jesus gave us favor and protected us…

God led us to live in a prime school district, and there was favor for me to get employment, good income with flexible time to care for family and promotions. Before I knew enough to even ask Him for things, He provided!!! I can NEVER thank Him enough for His continuing care, love and direction. Jesus is truly my Husband and Father; there is no person that identifies with me as He does. There is no better Husband and Father…

The Lord Takes Care of His People

Psalm 16:1 Protect me, God,
 because I trust in you.
2 I said to the L ORD *, "You are my Lord.*
 Every good thing I have comes from you."
5 No, the L ORD *is all I need.*
 He takes care of me.
6 My share in life has been pleasant;
 my part has been beautiful.
7 I praise the L ORD *because he advises me.*
 Even at night, I feel his leading.
8 I keep the L ORD *before me always.*
 Because he is close by my side,
 I will not be hurt.

*11You will teach me how to live a holy life.
Being with you will fill me with joy;
at your right hand I will find pleasure forever.*

Contact info:

Nancy Herrold
Bristol, Tennessee

E-mail: **scleich@yahoo.com**

Facebook: **https://www.facebook.com/nancy.leich**

CHAPTER 12

EMETERIA F VEGA

This is my life's testimony in my journey with Jesus…

How God changes my life from not believing Jesus as God, but just a mere man till He made me His beloved child. We are 7 in the family. Three of us are born again believers and 4 are leaders of Iglesia Ni Cristo Church in the Philippines. I got married at the age of 20, that marriage was a premature one, I don't know about it…

It stopped all my dreams in life from being an ambitious one, an achiever in school, a scholar in the university and an eldest in the family. I was a dreamer and I could still remember all my dreams and it came true even if my belief at that time was to the Father God alone. That was how my former religion taught me. Deep in my heart I truly believe in God. I was brought up in my grandma's house with all the love. She was a devout Catholic. She prayed for the dead people and had a rosary every 6 am and pm. She loved me so much. Until I was 10 years old I was under my grandma and grandpa's care.

My mom told me that when I was still a baby, I had a sickness that made them tired, as if everybody did not want to hear me cry because I always cried. Then one night my mom was in a deep sleep and she had a dream, in her dream she heard the voice to get certain roots from this plant and boil it. So my mom did it per instruction in her dream. So she let me drink that boiled herbal medicine, and since that time I was totally healed. I grew up on the farm, my father was a farmer and he trained me about farming, a good man that everyone in the community appreciated him. He was a hard working man and my mom was a super hard working business woman. My mom trained me in our family business in the market, wholesaling and retailing rice and corn, meat and dried fish in the salted fish section.

My first horrible experience that had me in fear of all men was this trusted man of my father on the farm almost raped me when I was still 4 years old. I could still remember, we went to town because it was market day and all of our produce was sold in our town. I was riding a horse with him, he asked my parents to bring me back home and my parents were following us while riding a horse with my younger brother. The horse was a means of transportation from the farm going into the town. That time, I jumped off from the horse and ran away from him hiding in the cogon grass. He called me until he got tired and he finally left. I had waited for my parents who followed us and then I came out from the cogon grass when I heard them coming. I told them everything that had happened. My father flared up with anger that he almost killed the man, and then the man ran away.

God blessed me with a good family, and all. We were known in our place because of our business. I was always a consistent honor student, a scholar in high school, an athlete and I love to sing. My mom was a choir member in the Catholic Church and my dad knew how to play the guitar. He taught me how to sing and play guitar when I was 9 years old. At the age of 15, I was almost raped again for the 2nd time. That time I already knew how to fight men because I joined a martial arts school. After a long training, I taught men. I even taught men when I had fear of men, really I'm so aloof and shy that when I had one boyfriend and that was my husband, who has also a very strong personality. I got married after graduation from the university, at the age of 20. I was raised up in a very conservative family. This marriage was a wrong one but I still consider it a blessing because I have the best children ever. I thought I would have freedom…

All my dreams were bound because I could not fulfill them because I was not allowed to work. I had to serve my husband only. God made a way for me to serve HIM. He brought us to a place where there was no church of Iglesia Ni Cristo. I met Jesus at the age of 22. The Assembly of God Church Pastors and members in Southern Leyte serenaded us because it was the birthday of my husband. Actually at first, I really didn't like the way that church worshipped God. They were very noisy and I said to myself, this is not of God! But the brethren kept on praying…

Since then, we attended this church and had a series of Bible studies in our home. It was not good that I criticized their way of worship but God used me in that ministry. I taught the children songs, and then hunger and thirst came into my life when a missionary from America came to conduct a crusade. I saw in his face, Jesus… As the one that I saw in the photos; the 3 day crusade was really amazing. Every time that missionary stood in the pulpit, I saw Jesus in his face and I started crying. His name was Joe Townsend, the one who baptized me and since then, I became very active in the church and there was a hunger and thirst in me that made me to draw nearer to HIM. I am really a dreamer and all my dreams come true. I prayed to be baptized and to speak in tongues. It happened when we transferred to another city.

The church announced fasting for 3 days and I said; I have joined so that I will be healed of that gastritis. Thank God I was healed after that 3 days fasting, the first time. Glory to God; Then, I believe in His word that says,

"By the stripes of Jesus we are healed!" I claimed it until now.

All that happened to my husband and my family, God revealed it to me; Even the calamities that had happened to my place and to other places in my country, when there was a flash flood like the one in Ormoc City. God revealed it to me in dreams but I was still innocent in that time, what I did was pray. All that happened at home when we were robbed, I dreamt and woke up because I heard people and saw them get all the goods in our store and how they got the money. They even wanted to kill me but the housemaids covered me. I had a dream that in the church were 4 dead persons and it did happen. I saw coffins and I saw cars outside the church and it happened. There was a time when we worshipped God in the church, I saw with my own eyes, the one playing the keyboards was all in black that I could no longer see him. I told one of our intercessors, and we prayed for him. It really happened that he was lost but God restored him, he answered the prayers. I even saw the father of my children, God told me to pray this prodigal son, and when I looked at him, it was my husband. There was a time, when we were still 45 days in Masbate in the year of 1990. In my dream, I saw snakes coming to me and as I was climbing the mountain with much difficulty; I saw in the field that my father was plowing and someone came and shot him. I shouted and came near to him and to my surprise I picked him up and it was my husband with blood on his body and killed by a man. That next evening, it happened. Since I had all these things that kept on bothering me, I asked myself who can tell me about all of these things that I was experiencing. When I asked some Pastors, they did not tell me any thing. What I did was pray...

In that time I was pregnant with my youngest son. I prayed to God and He told me in an audible voice, that he, my husband will not die. He was airlifted to Manila. There was confidence in my heart, and people asked me why I wasn't sad because the situation was hopeless. It was because I heard from the Lord, and he gave me the assurance that he will not die; even the doctor told me to get ready because it will only be by the miracle of God that he will not die. He was in the hospital that time; the guards of the company were with him. There were men who came to the hospital that evening; they said it was mistaken identity. We stayed in the private hospital in Makati for 25 days. His situation was hopeless. I told the doctor, he will not die, he will live, and that was what God had told me. The doctor told me it would take them 6 hours to get the bullet from inside his body. So, I fervently prayed that time without fear because I could hold onto what I heard from God. He isn't a liar, His words are all true! Suddenly, the doctor woke me up and said that I have to see my husband in the recovery room. He praised me but I rebuked him, telling him God did it all not me. Imagine, 6 hours and they made it in 3 hours only. My husband survived! In the hospital, many Christians prayed for him. I had seen the favor of God. No relatives helped us but God used people whom I didn't even know.

When my husband cheated on me, I saw it all in my dreams. I saw the face of the woman. But still I was faithful to him. But there was a time when I almost gave up, thanks be to God of His great love for me. In the church, I was in the music ministry for 25 years before I went to the mission field. I also joined the intercessory group, my Pastor mentioned me.

By the grace of God, I was hired in the school to teach, I only submitted my papers just for formality sake but I wasn't interviewed. But before that I had a dream that I was teaching in that school, where in that time I did not apply yet. Just a few months from my dream, there was an offer for me to teach in that school, Caraga Regional Science High School hired as a Mathematics teacher. The principal did not observe me. He was just watching me outside the classroom. I told her that I didn't know how to teach. I took up that course and took the board exam. I passed that so I will know how to teach my children. The principal said that I am a good teacher. I insisted and I told her that I don't know. The favor of God was amazing. The whole division office personnel and even the teachers got jealous of me because I was assigned right away in that school where all the students are scholars. It wasn't because of me but it was because of HIS favor. After my class, the superintendent wanted me to report to her office. All that I did was to pray for her. She told me all her experiences in life. I can't imagine the favor of God. She sent me to the national trainings. I was even given a scholarship in MA in music at the Philippine Women University, but my husband did not allow me so, I turned down the offer. The division office sent me to different trainings in NAMCYA (National

Music Competition for Young Artists), every summer to Baguio. In school I handled the choir for 10 years and joined the school division choir competitions, up to the National Competition.

  I was also a volleyball coach for boys and girls for 8 years. The school sent me to regional trainings and I became a regional officiating in volleyball. I gave up teaching mathematics in Science High, instead I taught music and values so that I can preach and do Bible studies every day. That time I was on fire for God and I made most of the opportunities to share the gospel as a leader in the campus ministry. I did Bible study in Values as an educational subject. I did not follow the books in Values; instead I got a book series of Bible studies from our church. It was the favor of God, the superintendent and the principal did not call my attention. The student's lives were changed. That time I decided to have a prayer meeting at home at 6 PM so I announced it during my choir practice and those who were under me in Values Education were coming to the daily prayer meeting at home.

  My eldest daughter who studied in Cebu City, Philippines was attending the Maranatha Church, called me, she told me to attend a 3 day River of Joy Conference in her church in Cebu. Her pastor is Pastor Joe Disarno, a missionary from the US. That was the turning point in my life. When we entered the room, I could not stand and I was drunk in the Spirit. When the worship team started singing I could no longer sing because I fell down till the end of the service. We were all laughing and crying. Even when the conference ended, I was still drunk. I went back to my city, I was in school, and it was as if I was floating. And I could hear a lot of voices, the voices of angels singing. When somebody is talking negative about me, I could see the mouth of this person who was backbiting me.

I heard the voice of God calling me, instructing me to pray and fast. After a week God told me to fast for 21 days, the following month for 40 days. Even when I was teaching, I obeyed the Lord. In my school my students noticed that I was filled with the power of the Holy Spirit. That is why I am accustomed to fasting while at work. I have time to meditate His words during recess and lunch break. My students noticed that my weight was reduced and they asked me if I was sick. Nobody can stop me; I obeyed the voice of God. I did the Bible study every day and prayer meeting every 6 PM. At first, there were 2 students who attended and stayed in the prayer meeting. But the Holy Spirit moved at that time and then the students who experienced Him broadcasted it to their classmates and schoolmates of what had happened in my house; until my whole house could no longer accommodate the size…

We started with the praise and worship and I was strumming the guitar, then all those who attended the meeting were filled with the power of the Holy Spirit as what we can read in Acts 2. They saw visions, angels, fire fall on them then, there the wind blew and we experienced the cold atmosphere. Later we smelled a nice perfume so that my whole house smells like it. There was laughing in the spirit and all the students in the meeting could no longer stand and the parents who came to fetch their children were also filled with the power of the Holy Spirit. Every night there was a new experience. When I started to lead worship with my guitar, the power of the Holy Spirit would fall and almost all who attended would just fall down without laying hands on them, when I passed by they just fell down. When I commanded fire to fall on them it hit the person who was open, when I commanded the wind to blow and it obeyed…

Students saw visions of an open heaven fall on them. One meeting, one of the prayer warriors stepped on nails and her right foot was swollen and we prayed and instantly it was healed that she could walk straight. We prayed with sick people, instantly God healed them all. People in the community invited us to have Bible study in their houses and sick people we also invited when going to their houses got healed when we prayed. Even if I just passed by them the people fell down; just by a command people fell down with no laying on of hands. No Pastors taught us, the Holy Spirit was our teacher. I just followed what the Holy Spirit said. Persecutions came but there was no fear because I knew it was all the works of the Holy Spirit. I did not even ask for offerings, everything was free during the meetings. No snacks were served but people came because they had seen the power of God! And those who were hungry and thirsty were filled with the power of the Holy Spirit. The religious spirit was broken, walls between denominations were broken and the non-denominational organization of Pastors and leaders was restored. We named it SECAMFEL. I was then informed that the Jesus Revolution Now movement headed by Pastor Jerome Ocampo was to come to our Solemn Assembly but he just sent leaders from another city which is very far from our city, since they were busy preparing for the Convergence. I headed the Solemn Assembly with the support of Surigao Evangelical Christian Fellowship (SECAMFEL) the first time that the Evangelical Churches were RESTORED for a long time there was a wall between the evangelical denominations in the province and city until now; Glory to God! We had a 6 AM – 6 PM prayer and fasting. I had a one day leave that time in school. I did not inform the students about the Solemn Assembly because I knew that the school would take action and have me face whatever questions asked by the parents. But many students attended without my knowledge, some were hiding…

I anticipated action from the parents but God gave me favor always because He was the one that is glorified and no church was being lifted up, only the name of JESUS.

One of the brothers of a student who attended in my house complained to the radio station. The principal was called, and she was told to call my attention. She interviewed the students, they told the principal it wasn't my fault, because I did not invite them to come to my house anymore...

I did not bring them to my church. I told them about Jesus. Only few knew that I was attending the Charismatic Full Gospel Assembly. One prayer gathering in church, my intercessors joined the prayer meeting, the people in the church criticized them and they stopped them. I got hurt that time because of the love of God in my heart I forgave them. Evangelism spread all over the school and community. The students handled the Bible studies teaching the children, I just gave them the pamphlets and they preached what the Holy Spirit told them, as I had already series of Bible studies in school before they were used by God, without studying, in the Bible school, many got saved.

Water baptism every Sunday afternoon was made by the Pastors, I did not initiate the water baptism because I hadn't enrolled yet in Bible School, I had no license to do it. The parents tried to control their children so they would not be baptized but they escaped and came by car to the sea where it was being done. Later, I enrolled in Bible class and a mission's course. To God be the Glory, 6 of my disciples graduated from high school they too decided to enroll in the Bible class. I and all 6 of them graduated the same year in the Bible school and mission course. One short term international mission trip of Jesus Revolution Now! They were sent by the church with me to Thailand. The Holy

Spirit led me in what was to be done in Thailand. In my second trip there was also the ministry I did when I went home to my city; we ministered to the prostitutes together with the Scandinavian Missionaries in Thailand. So, what we did in our short mission trip was also the leading ministry when we got home to my country.

So we prayed together with the prayer warriors, we had a Jericho March for 7 days. We started praying at 10 in the evening, after 7 days the walls were broken down and evangelism was opened. God sent us to the 2 leaders of the prostitutes who were also witches. We started in the house of the head of the prostitutes while it was going on, the prayer warriors were praying for me because I can't stand up and my eyes were closed as if I were drunk! Thank God! The whole family got saved. The Bible study and teaching of the children continued with the prayer warriors and me supporting financially. I entered the clubs and the pub houses because the prayer warriors were still under age, they stayed outside praying for me. I ministered to the prostitutes and some of them listened and got saved and stopped in their work. I had Bible study with them. Many stopped being a prostitute.

We declared that the clubs will be closed and it will be changed to a business area. It happened, glory to God. I was also present in the area where the Bible study was conducted by children every weekend.

The head in that community challenged me, she said, "This area is owned by the devil, why are you here?" Opening a Bible study, preaching Jesus was very dangerous, they said no, but Jesus loves the people in this area.

When we join the prayer meeting in the church, the people of that church will criticize them and stop them. I got hurt that time but because of the love of God in my heart I forgave. It never stopped me. Evangelism spread all over the school and the community. The students handled the Bible studies teaching the children. They had no training in the Bible school. I just gave them pamphlets I got from church. My choir members attended the Bible study every Saturday and the Barangay Captain gave us a place to hold these meetings reaching the less fortunate children. I used my money and everything for their snacks. Before the opening of school, I bought school supplies and gave it to the less fortunate students; I also sponsored those students who couldn't pay the school fees. I paid it. I got it from my salary. The students will come to me if they have no breakfast because they were poor. I let them get their snacks in the canteen. I helped also the orphans in our orphanage. I saved my salary for my international mission outreach in Thailand, Vietnam, Cambodia, and China. It is all by faith. As a Jesus Revolution Now Coordinator at the time, there was a convergence in Manila at the Araneta Coliseum. All the coordinators have special sessions with speakers like Dr Michael Brown, Lou Engle and Dr Cindy Jacobs, Che Ahn and the worship team of Rick Pino. That was one of my privileges, to listen to them in one closed door meeting. It was another encounter with the presence of God. When Dr Michael Brown spoke about Missions, in Araneta Coliseum, my heart and mind was focused on his teachings. There was hunger and thirst for more of HIM so, I listened carefully. When he had an altar call I ran in front and I cried out to God then, I heard the voice of God who told me,

"I will bring you to the nations," and after I shouted and said, "Yes Lord!" Dr Brown confirmed it by saying, "God has told you that He will bring you to the nations! Obey!"

After the meeting, I went outside and I signed up for my first mission trip to Thailand. I did not mind if it cost me all my money that I got from my salary. I started saving, selling my plants and all ways of accumulating money until I bought my first international ticket, not to mention my domestic air ticket as well. I was far from Manila and I have two air flights. And another problem was my ground fee. Pastor Charlie Carino, the coordinator of International Mission Outreach of Jesus Revolution Now had told us that the ground fee is $600. I had no doubt because when I took up the mission course, money was the number five qualification to go to the mission field, obedience is number one. I kept confessing that God will supply all my needs. At that time I was connected to the PDEA and had conducted the Provincial Anti-Drug Forum with the help of Pastors in my province. The effort and money I spent and all too just educate the people about drugs; how dangerous it is to the lives of the students. There were Bible studies and meetings with the Regional training of policeman. I got connected to the Regional Director who also supported me. Then, there was a follow-up Trainer's training of the leaders of the whole province of Surigao, student leaders in the city and province that was sponsored by the Provincial governor. They spent Ph 250,000.00 for this training, the fruit of our fervent prayers. Philippine Drug Enforcement Agency used me to connect to all the mayors and governors and even congressmen for a forum in every province and municipalities. I was still teaching at that time at the Department of Education, but I had to ask sometimes for a leave of 2 days just to go to the different places with the Philippine Drug Enforcement Agency, Regional Office personnel. My part was preaching the good news.

   They assigned me as the Mindanao Coordinator of Youth Power Against Drugs. If you are led by the Holy Spirit, there is nothing impossible with God. He was the one who directed and instructed me on what to do. He connected me to different people, through prayers they just can't say no when I ask help from them. They supported me. I didn't have fear, that time there was a serious drug problem in my country until now. My heart and mind was focused on God and His leading in my life. I did not even talk about it. I just obeyed God because I know many of my students were victims of it. Even the remotest area was infiltrated with drugs, pushers and users were everywhere.

In my mission trips God used people everywhere and even inside the airplane. I had seen God, his favor was so amazing. Imagine, I was preparing myself that time for my first international mission trip to Thailand. I attended the National Training on Education Against Drugs. I sang the song "Above All." While a Christian woman was taking a bath in the camp heard me sing this song. She asked me to stay in their house while waiting for the scheduled flight to Thailand. For one week, they supplied all my needs in their house for free and also my one month needs for the mission field. On our way to Thailand, the woman sitting next to me on the airplane was touched by God and she gave me $50 which was the money I used to buy gifts for some of the donors that I asked for in prayer before I entered the plane. That woman prayed for me and she told me to keep her informed through e-mail of my mission trip. The family provided all my needs in going back to my city. This couple brought me to Shoe Mart and gave me a free shopping spree, whatever I wanted to buy and then they brought me to a Thai restaurant ; Oh my God, everything in God's favor!

When I was already in my city, the Holy Spirit gave me a vision to mobilize Surigao Del Sur, another province in Mindanao for a Solemn Assembly. Just for a week, glory to God all the Pastors from different denominations were gathered in unity. And I informed Jesus Revolution Now in

Manila will be a big event! There were 800-1,000 people from all different places who attended; one from a tribe very far from the place where we were gathered. I saw that tribe in my dream so I expected them to attend, and they said that they left their place in the morning because they came by walking; a one day walk from the mountain. I brought also the music team from SECAMFEL, which were musicians from different denominations. Each one has to provide their own bus fare. It was all by faith. But the young people really love to go with me. Each Pastor was given a chance to pray in this Assembly. At that time revival took place. We were all filled with the power of the Holy Spirit another big event of JREV in Southern Leyte. JREV Manila called me to attend the Solemn Assembly and bring with me the music team of JREV Surigao, Maranatha Church, Cebu headed by Salome led this worship with the other music teams. So I told the team, those who are interested in going, they must have faith because nobody will shoulder their expenses. God provided everything, and they all enjoyed it. Thousands of people attended. They went and they experienced a move of God there. My team was the last one to worship then I was assigned for the closing prayer and declaring the victory. All were filled with joy when we went back to our city. All glory belongs to God.

My first trip to Thailand was in April-May 2006. Our team was named Zechariah, and we were assigned in Chaingmai, 10-12 hours travel from Bangkok to Chaingmai. We left the airport going directly to the bus terminal. Only a few were assigned to Bangkok. Almost all of us were assigned to the tribes. At first we ministered to the Thailana Church, Chaingmai. These were Bible School students in Tribes of the Nation Outreach (TNO) with my team there. There was an impartation of spiritual gifts to the students. Our team has a treasurer and we gave our ground fee for our food and transportation including all other expenses. We had a tracks distribution from house to house and we went to the Karen tribe. We did a Jericho march in the church. There was a bad spirit which threw a stone at my back while we were praying holding our hands together, I shouted at the top of my voice because of the pain but we could not find the stone. The enemy retaliated and that was always his work.

"Why me," I ask the Lord at this time?

Then we ministered to the youth, there was a revival in that church. The other teams were assigned in other tribes, they helped build a church, and some met with an accident. Even our Mission Director Pastor Charlie Carino, he was hospitalized due to an accident, and we were called to visit him in the hospital. So we visited and prayed for him that the broken part of his hand would be healed. The x-ray showed that his arm was broken and needs an operation. He was scheduled for an operation the following day. We were told to contribute money for the hospital bills. We prayed that Pastor Charlie will be healed. After our prayer, we left the hospital and went back to the Karen Tribe. We received a report from Pastor Charlie: he said that he will no longer be operated on because he was healed. All of us were happy and we thanked God…

The money we contributed was given back to us yeheey! Glory to God! We prayed for the sick people and they were healed. Then we went to the Lahu Tribe. There we went around the tribe with our interpreter. We were instructed to just smile at the people. And we went house to house to invite them to fellowship in the evening. In a small church made of cogon grass, without nice instruments, only our voices we lifted up praises to our God and some did warfare in unity and love, revival took place again in that tribe. Sick people were healed. After the meeting we went back to our accommodations and the next day we went to the children's house of the Lahu Tribe. Some swam in the brown stagnant water as if it were their swimming pool, while some of us prepared a special number and games. My work even if I am not told to pray, as a prayer warrior, I was always prepared; always at war wherever we go. Then we went back to the Karen Tribe for another revival meeting in the evening.

In our devotional prayer meeting in the morning, the presence of God was so strong. We seek His face and asked for His leading for us to minister. The secretary recorded all the revelations of the Holy Spirit. One of us saw elephants, then I heard the voices of children, and one saw a dragon with fire coming out of its mouth and fire blowing out its tail. We prayed hard after that and we agreed to buy oil to anoint each one of us and the gate of the school as well as the exit. Before we entered this school, we prayed in unity by the leading of the Holy Spirit as we saw already that at the gate there was a dragon blowing fire from its mouth. We held hands and prayed, and we anoint each one with oil, there was too much heat so we could not move our feet were stuck at the gate but in constant warfare because the enemy is defeated. And we were able to do a Jericho march in the playground. The Holy Spirit instructed us to go two by two, the other one will sing a song of worship and the other one will pray. For seven times, we went around their oval and at the exit we prayed because we saw the tail of a dragon with fire. We stood there and prayed and anointed the gait. Thank God He has given us the victory. Then we went to the principal's office, there we were entertained by the principal and we were brought inside the office. While he went out to instruct the one in charge in the canteen to prepare snacks for us; we all sprayed all the small and big Buddha's with oil, declaring the evil spirits in it, rendering them powerless! The favor of God made us go to the rooms of the schools where we met the students in each class and we were victorious. The next day, the host pastor told us to prepare because we will attend a wedding. Before we went back to Chaingmai, we will ride an elephant and we could take a bath at the hot springs. Then we went back to Chaingmai passing Shangri, where the border of Myanmar is located. We prayed over Myanmar.

All the team from the different tribes met at the Thailana Church for a revival meeting. Then we went back to Bangkok. We were riding a train and we were so happy and full of victorious testimonies. It was 13 hours of travel from Chaingmai to Bangkok. We stayed again in the same place, in the guest house. We went to the tourist destinations and enjoyed our last day of our stay in Thailand. We went to the Buddhist Temples and did warfare and put the oil to the Buddhist temples, declaring and warring against the evil spirits of all the Buddha's. We went to the temples making friends with the monks and led them to accept Jesus as their Lord and Savior. They also cannot resist, many of them accepted Jesus. See the power of God. Signs and wonders will follow those who obey HIM! All glory to HIM alone!

In July 2007, I went to Manila to attend the Jesus Revolution Now Convergence at Cuneta Astrodome. My ministry at that time was as an intercessor of this convergence! We woke up early at 4 AM to prepare ourselves for going to the Dome. One of the speakers was Prophet Tomi Fomirite, who instructed me to pray for the Pastor of Bangkok. Her instruction was to be obeyed while a camera man was videoing my prayer. I looked for that Pastor with the camera man with me. Thank God I found him, so I prayed for him. The 2nd day of the convergence, someone called me to go to the entrance. A group of gays wanted to join the convergence. They asked me to pay for their entrance fee. I invested in souls for his Kingdom, that's how God did to my heart. They joined and they all ran to the altar as the speaker called for the altar call. I was busy at that time, as an intercessor, I had to be in my place at the back of the speakers. After the convergence I went back to my city and to the same ministry with the youth.

Jesus Revolution Manila called me to attend the JREV Solemn Assembly in Kidapawan. It was a long travel of about 14 hours by land from my city. I had a stop over at the Davao City bus terminal for 5 hours, so I slept at the bus terminal, and left early to travel to Kidapawan. The coordinator of JREV in that place was the daughter of the congressman who fetched me and I stayed in their house. The whole day we cleaned the area and prayed for it. We also visited other churches and had prayed for revival. More or less 700 young people were gathered in the evening. It was raining the whole day and we asked God to stop the rain, He did it....

Thank God answers our prayers, the rain stopped. I was there to intercede. Afterwards I went back to work in my city via Cagayan de Oro. A whole day travel, in the bus I met the manager of a big bookstore in the Philippines. It was the favor of God and I told her that our orphanage needs books. She got my address, I prayed to God that she will help and release those books that I asked from her. God answered the prayer; amazingly, The President of the Charismatic Full Gospel Assembly called me that there were boxes of books sent to the orphanage. She was surprised because I did not tell her about it, but it was under my name... Glory to God!

In February 2007, I let the leader of YPAD (Youth Power Against Drugs) book us for a promo ticket for the next international mission trip of JREV to Thailand that was scheduled for April 2007 with the wife of a Pastor, a family friend of mine. Then I sent money to him amounting to Ph 25,000.00 for 2 persons but to avail the promo cost which was only Ph 12, 500.00 which was a 50% discount. I trusted him because I had helped him in his advocacy under the Philippine Drug Enforcement Agency. I checked the ticket by calling him once a week. So graduation in school was finished. I prayed in the church before I took leave. When I was in Cebu going to Manila, while eating lunch together with my daughter, I received a call from that youth leader.

He said, "I am sorry because I did not buy your tickets because I did not have the money." I was shocked!

This was always the words that I heard from God, "Be still my soul and know that I am God." This was a very terrible experience.

The wife of the Pastor was already in Manila as I was on my way to the airport. I was determined to go to Thailand. I called my sister and told her that the man did not buy our ticket but used our money. I told her that it wasn't the time to retreat but we have to go! She was convinced and bought the ticket again. The devil hindered us but he can't win. The air ticket to Thailand at that time was doubled in price. So I withdrew my last money in the bank Ph 25,000.00 for a round trip ticket. We did not sue him in court. We forgave him but I don't trust him anymore. He told me that, the advocacy where we started has now grown and it can't support my mission trips. He always asked me to pray for every event and I prayed.

In 2007, I went back to Thailand. Our team, named Samuel was sent to the Omkoi Tribe. We arrived from

Bangkok Monday morning. We waited in the staff house of the Korean Bible School of this tribe. I was with my disciples; they were the new graduates from the Bible School. The following day, we ministered to the children in the gym. A lot of young people got saved and those who were sick got healed. It was included in the plan that we will be sent to one of the churches of the Pastor from Thailand that I prayed for during the convergence in the Philippines. One of his churches on the other side of Omkoi was where Revival in Thailand had started. It was a small church where the light from heaven hit that church and all the tribal people came to this church to see the light. Thousands were gathered and worshipped without using an instrument. They just clapped their hands. It is where Revival in Thailand had started in the mountain. While waiting on the head pastor of that church, we prayed and in deep worship the Lord said that on Thursday we will go to that place. That day was Monday. So while waiting for that day a missionary from Australia fetched us and brought us to another tribe, where there was a youth camp. We prayed on the playground, we applied the blood of Jesus. In the evening we ministered to the young people. More than 500 young people were touched by the fire of the Holy Spirit. They saw visions, they prophesy, they spoke in tongues and they saw angels ministering. The next day, we woke up early and prayed on the playground where the children will do their exercise. But we saw bees fly out from the Buddhist Temple going to that playground. That time the campers were still inside the church praying. We prayed, we rebuked but the bees were still there. It occupied the whole ground. The team gathered again to seek His face and ask forgiveness because we did not ask guidance of the Holy Spirit first. The second time we prayed and the Holy Spirit instructed us to go two by two in each corner of the playground, and then we rebuked the bees to disappear.

The bees went to the center of the playground and it became a black pig.

My disciples said, "Oh my God!" in a loud voice that made the black pig go out of the ground and disappear. Glory to God!

What a lesson we learned.

We have to put our trust in the Lord and lean not on our own understanding in all our ways we have to acknowledge Him and he will direct our path. Proverbs 3:5-6

God will not answer our prayer when we have to do things on our own. We finished the youth camp preparing the team to go to another tribe, we went back to our accommodations that evening, and we traveled in the middle of the night with Australian Missionaries. Thursday afternoon, we traveled to the other tribe to see the place where Revival first took place in Thailand. The head Pastor and our team met. We stopped where the light from heaven hit that church. I was talking to a man, I really forgot him.

He said Sis Emie,"You will see the place and the intercessors in my church."

I asked his name and he reminded me of that time that I prayed for him during the JREV convergence in the Philippines.

I said, "I am sorry," he is the Pastor of the mega church in Thailand.

That church where we went was one of the tribal churches. He brought a woman that met with an accident in Bangkok, coming to the place where we were going. We arrived at 6 pm in the evening. Our things were brought to a house where we stayed and we went right to the church to pray for a woman with the intercessors. Amazing the youngest intercessor is only 4 years old and the oldest is 12 years old. We started praying at 7:30 pm and we never stopped. It was videoed until 3:30 am. We saw the wound closed miraculously. Sunday morning I was assigned to preach in the house where the children (intercessors) were waiting. There were sick people, who attended that meeting I preached about the blind man, but it wasn't done because the Holy Spirit led me to sing the song, "Here I am to Worship." As I strummed the guitar, the Holy Spirit moved mightily and the sick people worshipped with us and they walked, jumping and were praising God! The house had an earthquake, an intensity of 8 which was the power of the Holy Spirit. Glory to God! What an awesome presence of God...

The children prayed like machine guns! All of us were blessed with those children. Then we went to church with intercessors and there the service had started, the presence of God was so strong. During the altar call the Holy Sprit moved and filled the church with His awesome presence...

After all the works in that tribe we went back to our accommodations and that was a long travel. You know in the mission field God will give you His all sufficient grace, strength so that you will not get tired. I even massaged the missionaries. Last day in Omkoi I was told to cook Pork Adobo. That was a funny experience. I went to the market to buy vinegar. It is so hard, they did not know what vinegar was; I had to show the sales lady by facial expression. Still, she didn't get it and I went back without vinegar. I cooked Adobo without vinegar, but it was still okay. The team had a medical outreach in the gym. A lot of sick people came and were ministered to by the medical team. The next day we went back to Chaingmai and had a revival meeting at the church in the evening. The following day, the 700 Club wanted to interview each one of us but we heard from the Pastor that the Buddhist leader was looking for us because of the revival that happened in the Youth Camp in the Omkoi Tribe. So, we were told not to go out that day. The next morning, we went to the house of a well known witch doctor. The spirit was so strong and there was a foul odor that we could smell. Again we prayed that the witch will allow us to get inside of his house, as we declared, it happened. He could not say no. There in his house we laid hands on his big and small idols and rebuked the evil spirits, we ministered to him and he accepted Jesus as his Lord and Savior, a powerful work of the Holy Spirit. We said good-bye to Chaingmai. The next day, in the afternoon we traveled by train for 13 hours, going back to Bangkok. We stayed in the hotel and we enjoyed the last day of our stay in Thailand. We went shopping and then went to the airport. We arrived safely in Manila after 3 hours travel. Good for those who are living in Manila they could go direct to their houses but for me, I still had to travel by plane for 2 hours. So I went to the mission house, rested for a day and then traveled back to my city.

After my mission trip to Thailand, we had a national youth camp. The leader, had an altar call, the all nations' flag was lining the front rows, and the leader told the campers to fall in line to stand at the flag where they wanted to do missions work. You know what? Almost all the campers fell in line in front of the US, Canada and Australian flags. After 3 months, there comes an offer from my friend in Manila to see if I am interested to go to China. I asked my mentor, the President of our church CFGM, and she said, "Okay!" So I filed a 6 months leave from school…

I was granted my leave. Two teachers went with me. We bought tickets from Manila to Macau. God made a way for us. When we were at the border of Macau going into China, there was a long line. I was stopped by the policeman and brought to the head of the border. He threw my passport in front of another officer, but I wasn't afraid. God gave me boldness to defend myself for any reason. I didn't know what was my fault, so I asked the officer at the border,

"Why did the policeman show disrespect to me and throw my passport?" In boldness, I commanded the policeman to pick up my passport. To my surprise, he obeyed. I said to myself, "thank God!"

The police officer just smiled at me and he asked me if I am still single. I told him directly to just look at my passport. I told him that I wanted to visit his country, I even told him to please release me now because my companions are waiting outside for 30 minutes. I was not detained for interrogation. I thank God for His wisdom. It was the biggest issue so far and thousands were falling in line there. We arrived in China that evening. We stayed in the hotel and the agents told me that I will not be accepted in school because I am too old; I was 42 at that time. I rebuked her because I don't want to hear negative words. We got connected to the Nigerian Church. We attended services during Sundays. We rented a condo unit with the help of the church and we ate outside. One teacher had started her work, and the other teacher was denied because of her health condition. For me, I was still praying, and applying. Thank God I found a school, Yinyin Kindergarten School and a tutorial studio in South China Normal University. It was really favor from God, a nice school. It was really arranged by God. But 2 of my companions went back to the Philippines. I was the one left. Forty days waiting for my salary, all my money was just enough for my fare going to school, for food and I have to wait for one month till the school gave me free meals. I was forced to fast for 15 days. Every Saturday, I ate food in the church during our practice in praise and worship, until Sunday. I prayed and cried out to God to strengthen me and keep increasing my faith every day. In school, one morning while going down the stairs, I saw miracles. I saw money flying in the air and I caught it…

This money was enough for my needs till my pay day. I thanked and praised God, I shouted to the top of my voice. Some of the students and teachers came out from their rooms. Chinese people helped and supplied my needs for food and winter clothes miraculously, I snatched a woman who almost fell down from a bus while the door was still opened, and the driver did not see her because of so many passengers. I was near the door and it wasn't locked yet so she fell down and I reached out my right hand. Since that time, we became good friends and all that I prayed to God regarding my food was answered. I didn't know how to order food in the restaurant (language barrier). After church service we went to different restaurants with delicious food they served. During Christmas I received a Bible from my employer, it was a miracle. It was translated in English and Chinese. I was amazed. A communist employer gave me a Bible? We cannot even carry a Bible there in China.

Another one that amazed me was when I encountered an angel, he helped me when I was lost, I did not find the bus stop and nobody knows how to speak English to help me. I wrote words in my cell phone and showed it to them and still they shook their heads and said they didn't know. It was almost an hour of waiting and praying until a tall man appeared in front of me, I told him about my problem. He brought me to the bus stop, it was still very far and it was a long walk. He told me to follow him, and when we arrived at the bus stop and he gave me money and he said okay the bus is coming. He went away smiling at me. He disappeared. I smiled above and said my heartfelt thank you to Jesus. In that rented condo, I talked to Jesus alone.

During winter, I didn't have a heater in my room. But I made myself warm with 6 layers of clothes which I wore. I did not complain to God, I knew that HE was the one who brought me here and I just followed what HE put in my heart. In 2008, there was an order from Beijing that all expats will go home and that the school will no longer allow an English teacher to teach. April 2008, they closed all the embassies in Macau, Hong Kong and all the neighboring countries. My visa at that time expired on April 24th, 2008. That was because of the upcoming Olympics. My partner in teaching English, who is from Canada, left me in January. The school didn't want me to go and they adopted me. The police car was the one who brought me to my accommodations because in the bus the policemen checked all of it. My photo in the school was taken.

The parents just told me, "We like you Emie and the children do too, that is why we don't want you to go."

But I bought a ticket online in secret and went back to the Philippines because I heard a lot were captured and put in prison for deportation. Exactly that date: April 24, 2008, I was already at the airport and I called my employer. When I arrived in the Philippine Airport I called my employer again. Together with the children, they shouted"

"We miss you Emie, please come back!"

But I did not come back but instead I went to Cambodia.

Our point of entry to Cambodia was Vietnam. There we met the Pastor and his wife. They rented a house and made it a school for small children. It is very strict in Vietnam, when they saw people gathered in one place or in a house; the neighbors will make a report right away to those who are in authority. We ate the food they prepared and immediately we left the place bringing our food because the policeman came. We saw a little time in Vietnam; we went to their museum that caused pain in my heart. I saw photos during the Vietnam War. In the tunnels, orientations were made. There was a short film showing. We saw how the Vietnamese won the war against the US. We went into the tunnels and prayed while crawling inside while having warfare. There were tunnels that measured 50m. That made me almost collapse inside of it. Then we went to the bus terminal taking a bus ride to Cambodia. In the border we did warfare, praying that not one of us would be left behind. Some had been checked and asked by the police officers. After crossing the border, we traveled to Cambodia in peace and full of joy. We arrived to the orphanage late at night. All of us were instructed to bring something from the Philippines, to be given to the orphans. The orphans were told to fall in line on the stairs waiting for the things that we will give to them. My backpack was full of food and things. Each one of us gave to the orphans. We ministered to them, we prayed and we felt so much pain in our hearts when we embraced them. We went again to another orphanage where the young people lived. We ministered to them, we prayed for them, and showed them the love of God for them. We shed many, many tears…

We went to one of the secondary schools that were made as camps for the prisoners, where they tortured and made man as a barbeque. So much pain we felt there, it was agony. The last place that we visited before we went to our assigned workplace was the killing field. It is far from the city…

My God! At the time that we entered that place, those who had the Gifts of the Spirit saw, smelled and heard the cries of the people. The skulls were piled in a glass house that all could see it and there were hairs, dresses, shoes, pants, etc. That place was where the victims were tortured, the women were raped and men were killed, young and old…

We went back to the orphanage. We had our fellowship together with the orphans and teachers in the school owned by the Australian Missionaries. The following day, we bid goodbye to the orphans, and we went to our assigned place. There were teams sent by tribes. My team was sent to the school. It was owned by a Christian Church. We were given an accommodation there. We slept in the kindergarten classroom with the mat and a pillow of the children and with only a ceiling fan in the room. At first our body got pained because we slept on the floor which is hard and there was no foam. Later we got adjusted to it. We had no mosquito net either. Our things were up in the room where we climbed up into a tree which we enjoyed. It was all for Jesus. I taught the grade one pupils, and the adult ones. We helped the teacher take care of the children, feeding them during lunch time. During the weekend we have to get ready to lead a Bible study. I shared with them my knowledge in music, to the praise and worship team. We brought our own food, cooked and shared with them. We made ourselves a blessing to the church by contributing to the needs of the church.

In the evening we would go to their park and do a prayer walk and see the place. The Pastor treated us by bringing us to restaurants. Then we went also to the Widow's Island where we prayed and encouraged all the widows. I was assigned also to lead a Bible study with my fellow workers in His vineyard. We worked all day in a very uncomfortable place because we were still adjusting to the weather and everything else there. Thank God for His sustaining strength. He is really amazing and faithful to those who obey Him. We wash our clothes in the evening. We would finish in a month and the last days we went to SEAM REAP which we always enjoyed. It was a 2 day stay; we had a prayer walk and warfare in the Kingdom. Then, we went back to Vietnam. We stayed in the hotel this time. I went to the kitchen and shared Jesus with the chef and she accepted Him. Many of them went to my room for a massage for free. God gave me the strength to do it. They were all young ladies…

We enjoyed the night market, purchasing their food and we bought Kipling bags, wallets and North face backpacks, Adidas, many name brands etc. that were for my business. Then we traveled back to the Philippines.

In 2010, I went back to Cambodia; the same ministry in the school, glory to God. There was an amazing increase of students in the school. The last day, we had a teacher's retreat. That was an awesome spiritual encounter with the Holy Spirit. Then we were on our way back to Vietnam. We love to see the amazing motorcycles. How does the driver manage to carry things on his back? It was so nice to see all that were riding in those motorcycles. Their taxis were in a car but for long distances only. We had ministered with the young people. The Pastor brought us near the river bank with 60-70 young professionals and students. The Mission Director wanted us to transfer the venue of meeting to the Pastor's house. Two of us and the Pastor's wife who was our driver of this motorcycle was left behind, which would be our last trip. I discerned that there were policeman following us. I told the Pastor's wife to go another way and she said no and that there were no policemen spying on us. I said the policeman just crossed and he hit our motorcycle. God protected us and I saw that he was coming to hit our motorcycle, and I saw and rebuked him. A little bruised in the hands of the driver and all of us fell but we got back up right away and pulled the motorcycle and drove back to the church. Angels helped us as if we were all floating as we fell to the ground. We arrived at the meeting place, and we told them what happened to us. This was the spirit of retaliation…

The meeting was stopped because we knew the policemen were following us and everyone went on their own way out of the house and went home. We went to the boutiques as if nothing had happened. The policeman's motorcycle, as I saw it was divided and broken because it hit the corner of the road. The policeman rolled with blood on his head.

Back to school May – June 2010, July I and my co-teacher who was also my disciple left for Manila. The agency had called us for an interview regarding our application in one of the Philippine International Schools in Riyadh. After a long waiting, we flew to Riyadh, December 24, 2010 and we arrived December 25, 2010. We looked for a church right away. I attended an old Filipino church where the Head Pastor was put in prison together with his assistants. But the Head Pastor was the one who was deported. I prayed to God about that church. He told me to help and work with His servants to rebuild the church. The music ministry had been attacked by the devil. I talked to the Pastor there that he needs to raise up intercessors and the worship team should be prayed for and all the ministries of this church. The Assistant Pastor sent a letter to my school requesting the Principal to allow me to stay out starting Thursday evening until Friday. Thank God the principal approved but on condition that the school will not be liable for whatever will happen to me.

Wednesday evening we had a prayer meeting which we started just the 5 of us and 2 Pastors, their wives and a deacon. It was announced in the church during the service that there is a prayer meeting going on, those interested could join but that they have to come every Wednesday. And a choir practice every Thursday evening. Many responded and attended, and the young people got excited about the choir practice. They let me lead the praise and worship; the choir and prayer meeting. Glory to God, the attendees of the prayer meeting reached about 50 and up. We gathered in a secret place of the church and our cell phones were off. One or two cars were parked outside the house church. Some members are staying in that house.

There was a revival meeting of all the churches in Riyadh and the speakers were from the US and those brave enough got listed. Five of us in the church attended this meeting. The revival meeting was very far from the city because the venue in the Kingdom was cancelled. Thank God the meeting was pushed through and more than 8k true believers from different countries working in Riyadh attended this meeting. The meeting was awesome. We saw men and women and most were wearing their ABAYAS. (a full-length, sleeveless outer garment worn by some Muslim women). In school, the teachers knew me because of my disciple in the Philippines, who was also a teacher. There were times that I was called by my co-teachers because of the presence of bad spirits. They saw white ladies and black ladies. So I went and cast them out by the blood of Jesus and the spirits were defeated. I was assigned for the first 3 months in the kindergarten. I started my class with an opening prayer. One parent called the principal's office. She referred to me as the new teacher who prayed using the name of Jesus. But I did not listen. Still I prayed in the name of Jesus. During the Parents-Teachers meeting, the principal assigned me to sing the Doxology song and prayer. One Muslim stood up and protested. He said that they must be given top priority when it comes to prayer because Riyadh was theirs. It is the capital city of Saudi Arabia. I was the Glee Club advisor in school, so I had my choir again. I practiced with them all the gospel songs. At first, I preached to them with the lyrics of the song. I asked the principal if I would be the one to handle the values education subject in grades 9 and 10. It was granted. I did not follow the book but instead I gave my students the schedule of Bible study, prayer meetings and practice of worship songs. A Christian student played the keyboard. It happened and revival took place in two classes. In grade 9 and 10, students saw visions, they spoke in tongues and some saw angels. There was an intense heat of fire fall down on their heads from heaven. It just went on and on...

It was almost two hours in the presence of God filling the two classrooms. I lay hands on them; we were busy going from one class to the other class, explaining to the students what was happening to them. But before it happened, I had a film showing about JESUS from my laptop, I downloaded it from the deacon of the church. My Bible was in my cell phone. I had several students in that school learning piano and I had Bible studies with them during lunch time at the quadrangle but we couldn't get close to one another because the guard was always watching us. One of my students in piano class in grade 9 was the daughter of the supervisor working in the US Embassy, who accepted Jesus. We had a series of Bible studies through our cell phones. The school principal asked me about it but I told him the truth. Then I was sabotaged by the other teachers, who got jealous. Actually there was an injustice that I saw in the school, they did not pay us during the summer time and we were just given $400 per month which was not what we signed on for in our contract. I told them that when I go home I will no longer come back because there was so much pressure from the staff of the school. The favor of God was with me. He gave me the best certificate. And because of that certification he was out of that school and he is now teaching in the US. I sued them in court because there was an injustice done to all the teachers. I had tutorials outside my school, 10 of them and two in the church whom I taught the flute to. After a month they can already play in church. Most of my students in piano were Sudanese. Two of them were daughters of the lawyer of the Prince. I played the Christian music in their house; even the owner of the big hospital in Riyadh. I taught his daughter piano. That was how the Holy Spirit led me in that country. That was really the favor of God.

I had also a tutorial with the grandchildren of BABA; he was a Matawan, a widower and a Muslim police. He was a very rich man who owned a big construction company in Riyadh. There was a party like a farewell party the day before I left Riyadh. The offer was really good: they brought into the room jewelries and money of his wife. Baba and the children said that all will be given to me. I will be the owner of a big construction company with more than 300 workers and that my children will work in this company. Baba gave a box of chocolates and dates for my children. When I arrived to the Philippines, Baba kept on calling and asking me to send my papers because we will have a vacation in Italy together with his children. I just told him I am still enjoying my vacation, I did not want to hurt any people so I respected and answered his calls. Besides, he is a well respected man in Riyadh. Until this time I decided not to answer and I did not even tell him I work in Bahrain. I am protecting my calling, not my relationship to any man.

I went back to the Philippines, into my city. There were missionaries from the US, a group of basketball players and a medical team. I was the one who coordinated the team assigned to the school as well as the basketball team. I sent letters to all of the schools in the city with the approval of the superintendent. The missionaries ministered to the students in all the schools except the Catholic school. I brought the basketball team first to my school. There was a sports clinic attended by the varsity team in school for free. And the missionaries were able to minister to all students. Thousands of students got saved. Medical missions were also conducted, medicines were given for free and all the services for the sick people were free.

After this event, I was invited by one of the Pastors who coordinated the JREV Solemn Assembly in Surigao Del Sur. He is Pastor Robinson; there was a revival in their church with the youth and at that time the church was still small. The Pastor asked me to pray to God to raise up millionaires in the church that could support the ministry, and the prayer was answered by God. And without my knowledge, until the next time I was invited again, to come and speak to the youth of his church. The word that the Holy Spirit put in my heart that time of my preaching was:

"Enlarge your territory." It came to pass.

So I traveled from my city to his town for 6 hours by bus. I was amazed about what God had done for his life and the church. I asked the tricycle driver to bring me to Pastor Robinson's church and he brought me another way so, I insisted that it wasn't the right way to his church. The driver said that they had transferred already to their NEW big church. Oh my God! It was a big church...

But I did not ask, I just observed. He brought me to the hotel, where I stayed and his children came back to fetch me to return to the church on a tricycle. He asked me to pray and declare that the tricycle will become a Crosswind Car, as he desired it for his ministry. God answered our prayers for millionaires; the member that accommodated me when I first came to his church, now owns a hotel, a gasoline station and their construction supply. The second time that I was invited, Pastor brought me to their house and let me pray for the family. The church had enlarged their territory and had the church built near the hotel of the millionaire family. He invited me to speak before his church and revival took place. And they joined the JESUS REVOLUTION Convergence in Bagiuo. They experienced the move of the Holy Spirit. The speaker at that time was Dr Cindy Jacobs, Lou Engle, etc. At that time I was in China.

I was home at that time on vacation. I was under mentorship that time of Dr Cindy Jacobs in prayer. I was closely listening to her on video, discussing the topic of prayer. Suddenly the bombing of the Boston Marathon in Massachusetts happened. Two Muslims used homemade grenades. She instructed me to focus my prayer on that problem and I watched the news on CNN, BBC and Fox News so I can follow up in prayer. I monitored this and prayed all day. God answered the prayers.

April 2013, I attended the National Convention in my church. Pastor Charlie Carino sent me a message, asking me to prepare for a mission trip to the Province of Comval. The JREV team from Manila went to Compostela Valley, a province in Mindanao, to the place where the flash flood had happened and killed thousands of lives. This was such a horrible catastrophe. That place is far from the sea but there was a tornado that brought water into that place. We ministered to the Pastors, leaders from different denominations; they were united because of this terrible calamity. The Evangelical churches had their early dawn prayer every day. We ministered to the youth and also to the victims. Sad stories we heard from these victims, sad testimonies. Tents from different countries were given and small houses were given for free to the victims. There, we joined with them in their dawn prayer. Restoration and transformation of this place happened. Revival took place because they got united now and they humbled themselves and prayed. Signs and wonders followed those who went. Even the rain obeyed to stop when we prayed. After a week of ministry we had fellowship of feasting in our sister's house in Davao then I went back to my city which was 10 hours travel from Davao by bus.

Pastor Noel from Kulambogan, Lanao del Norte, Mindanao invited me as a guest speaker in his church for their first anniversary to the King of Glory. I traveled from my city for almost 16 hours by bus and boat. It was an awesome experience. God showed up in the meeting. Many were filled with the power of the Holy Spirit, Glory to God! Pastor Charlie, the JREV mission coordinator was also invited. My second time of invitation and when I go home for vacation, he will gather the pastors in his province for a revival meeting. I said in his perfect time, the name of Jesus is lifted up!

In the same year, 2013 I was in Manila with one of the schools, a Christian school while waiting for my visa to Vietnam. I already resigned from my school in the Philippines when I was still in Riyadh. No fear but by faith God provided everything. My ministry in school was to preach every first Friday of the month and I did this. I was also given a chance to one of the judges in BULLPRISA in the musical competition of all the private schools in Bulacan. Till the competition of all private and government schools, I helped the church in the music ministry.

   One day a friend of mine, a lawyer who owned the agency told me that one of the Royal Court Ministers in Bahrain wants me to teach his children. That was December 2013. So I tried and when I arrived there in their house, the environment wasn't good because it is not a school. Shaikh told me that I will get adjusted to the environment later. He introduced me to his other children which were from his other wife. Each child has their own nanny and I will not work as a nanny because I was hired as a teacher to his children. In my one week stay, the enemy hit my right foot so that I could not walk but thanks be to God for his favor. I was brought to the hospital and the doctor advised me to have complete bed rest for 3 days. The madam did not allow me so I showed her my medical certificate. She wanted me to sleep in the ironing room which I insisted was too hard. I told her that it was not good for my health and so I have to sleep in the guest room. She kept her mouth shut! She was shocked that there was someone who did not obey her. What was in my heart, I didn't do wrong and she has to respect me as the teacher of her children. I sensed that the wife was jealous of me. She insisted I do a massage to her husband but I told her I only massage women. The boss asked me to try me to massage him and I obeyed him and I applied pure Aloe Vera on him that I made from the plant, I did that in the presence of his wife. I knew deep in my heart that it was a way to test my heart. He had proven that God is with me.

It wasn't good but I took advantage of that time, I spoke in tongues while doing the massage, that made him obey and respect me, I prayed for him for 1 year. He doesn't want it but I knew that he was trying to test me. Many times I thank God for the strength and boldness in my spirit. One time, his wife wasn't in the house, he called me but I did not listen to him. The housemaids called me so as I respected him by being my boss as it says in the Bible, that we have to obey our employer even how harsh they are to us, so I went to their room. Oh my God! Really there was too much strength that God had poured out on me. The church knew how difficult it would be for me to escape this house. My passport is with the administrator. Since my visa had ended already last December 28th, I was reminded by them last November. They wanted to renew my visa with many promises. I did not tell them yet that I will have my vacation to the US and that I am praying now that when I apply, it will be approved. I heard that they don't allow anybody to go to the US; instead they will allow you to go back to your country instead. I did not inform them yet, because they will make problems for me and still the school year had not ended but will be over at the end of June.

Now, they will no longer allow me to go to school because they knew that I have sisters from the church who are working there and they are afraid that I will apply. Before there was a school who offered me a visa and will bring it when I go home but I wasn't allowed to go out without someone else with me. When I went to the mall, the driver is always at my back that brought all my things. They always do this to the other workers at home, those who disobeyed them; they will make problems for them. That is how they will treat you if they like you so much. He promoted me to be coordinator. I did all the conferences in schools and talked to the teachers. I was trained in this house; my patience has been stretched, teaching all these hyperactive children. Before they slapped me, spit on me, shouted at me and all. Now, they love me and they really don't want me to go. My feelings are attached to these children. I get along with them, with the support of the father and mother, but I am avoiding whatever things that get me in contact with him. I told myself, this is just a normal feeling because I was with them for 4 years and 2 months.

The children now have ambitions in life. They know now their responsibilities of being a student. I taught them to respect and obey their father but not to fear him to love their parents, their brothers and their sisters. Before their parents told them that they are not brothers and sisters but cousins but now they do not tell them this. I gave gifts and greetings during their birthdays. It means so much to them. Even the giving of their report cards, I taught them to give it to their father, explaining to them everything. There have been a lot of changes that God has done and still doing in this house. I told them that I love them with the love of Jesus. Before when I spoke in tongues, they would react right away and told their parents. But now they want to know more. Before they wanted me to convert to Islam with millions of Dinars in exchange for my faith but now they no longer tell me anything.

The boss has a good heart and is humble. Love is a powerful weapon. God is love and it conquers all. God is powerful and He will make all things beautiful in His time. Madam has changed a lot in the way she treats me. They are rich and with nothing more to do but to spend their money. They are not giving me a salary that is due me, even if the children are now getting excellent grades. But I did not mind it because I didn't do anything that made me disobey God. Fighting for my rights through prayer was the weapon of mine which defeated all the attacks of the enemy. It is really true; the house was full of evil spirits. The lust of the flesh; I was tried, tempted in every way up until now, the enemy did not give up. My God, temptation wasn't an ordinary one; it is really true that satan will not tempt us with just ordinary things. But thanks be to God for the intercessors who prayed for me so hard. I almost gave up! The hardest temptation that I ever experienced in my life is when my heart is the one being tested. Thank God I won. Glory be to His wonderful name. The Holy Spirit talked to me in a still small voice, what if you gain the whole world and lose your soul. Another one was the owner of a big school where I met at the pharmacy, who offered temptation again.

Another experience was that I was harassed by a policeman, the guard in the house of the Prince, I ran inside the house and I was almost cornered near the playroom. His gun scratched my hands. Thank God for His wisdom, he taught me how to escape away from the man. He knew that I was alone, and the family went away to their resort. I did not go with them because it was Friday and my time to go to church. The policeman said that whatever I will ask of him for help, he will do it and will I forgive him. He cried and asked forgiveness, so I forgave him. Every where in the house there is a camera which is connected to all the police stations. Even in the road there is a camera because it is a house of a Minister. The administrator teased and told me that I have a kind heart and I said because of Jesus I forgave him…

In the first church that I attended in Bahrain, I had a choir, and I joined the music ministry. After church, I went to the mall and had a prayer walk, and shared Jesus with my compatriots and to some Muslims. I made friends with them. Wherever I go I shared Jesus. I went to the dental clinic, I met a compatriot of mine, I shared Jesus but it so happened that she was a Christian in the Philippines. I called her every day, prayed for her, and asked her to attend church. The family attended. And the children are active in the music ministry as tambourine dancers. Glory to God; souls are just waiting for us. I up until now have a Bible study, prayer meeting through the cell phone. I have one in the US also. The harvest is ripe but the laborers are few. All busy bodies are looking for living and material things, perishable things; this is what I have seen. I do not compare myself to them, I just work and work for God. Because that is how I love my God because HE first loved me which helps me to love those that Jesus loves. There were those people, whom I helped, but they were stabbing my back, I don't care about this. I just prayed and forgave them. Because that is how Jesus works in our lives. I prayed to God to bring me to a church where I have freedom to worship Him in Spirit and in truth. I went to the nations obeying His call with all my money, I worked and fed myself; all by faith without complaint. I thank God for the children here, they have changed a lot and even the mother, she changed a lot. So now I am praying that He would enlarge my territory to a good place after rigid training, purging and all…

This is the first time in my life that I am teaching from Kindergarten up to grade 7. I am teaching Math, English, Science, Music and Art, ICT and French. Thanks be to God for His wisdom. I know, God is the one always glorified. Even the many times my boss has said that he truly appreciated my work, it is because I worked for God, not to please people even if there is much opposition.

The last testimony that God made a miraculous work in my family, when the father of my children got sick last month and he had a minor heart attack. He was brought to the hospital. My children called me and they cried, they wanted me to come home, I said that I can't. All that I did that time was pray. I got my guitar and worshiped God and prayed fervently on Wednesday. Then I heard the Holy Spirit tell me in a still small voice that they will go home on Monday, next week. My son took over the place of his father and that was why he was in my city. Since my daughter is also a youth leader in the music ministry in the church, she took over my place. There were many people there who prayed for him while he was in the hospital; many thanks to those who prayed.

After hearing the voice of God, I called up my son and told him: "Don't you worry, God said that your dad will go home on Monday."

But the relatives had lots of negative reports which I rebuked them all and cancelled in Jesus name. My son confirmed to me that surely they will go home on Monday according to what the doctor said. Glory to God; He is our Jehovah Rapha and by faith, all things are possible with God.

I can't even understand myself and all the people around me, only my mentor Rev. Marilou Navarro, the President of CFGM, understands me. She also told me, the only thing that I can give you are my prayers and the prayers of my church. I really respect this Woman of God! Never in my life have I ever seen a woman like her. She pushed me to become a leader. She knew how God used me, even my ups and downs. She knew me, my defender and my intercessor, Glory to God! I am always in communication with her, she always says YES if it is God's work. She gave all her life to Jesus. She is single. All I did was follow and still depending on His leading, Jesus taught me because nobody trained me like the other church had been doing. Yes, I graduated from our Bible school and was ordained as a

Pastor and had a certificate in the Mission course under Missionary Max Chismon. The wisdom I got all came from Him. I knew that when we fully surrender our lives to Jesus, He will be your everything; but it doesn't mean to say that we no longer need training. That is why I always say that I want to be trained and I want to know more of Him because there is hunger and thirst in me that only Jesus can satisfy.

I am always praying to God that He will bring me to another place where I can work fully, not one family only, like the one I am doing now. I want them to release me. How many times I asked permission to go but my boss just told me, "NO!" he said my children need you. I know that this is an injustice, but I leave it all up to Jesus. Yes, favor is there but I sensed in my spirit that always says, enough! There is a lot of work to do outside more than inside the house. So I am asking for all of you to pray for me...

I want to go to the United States of America.

There is a sign after praying, I asked by my best friend to sponsor me, and she said YES and my cousin told me that she will sponsor my air ticket. So what I have to do now is apply for the tourist visa. Now I am preparing a job letter and have my boss to sign it. That is one of the requirements of getting a tourist visa. Please help me in this. I am entirely living by faith.

Jesus said, "If my name will be lifted up I will draw all men unto me."
All Glory and honor belong to Jesus alone!

My favorite scriptures are:

Joel 2:28

God's Spirit Poured Out

28 "And it shall come to pass afterward
That I will pour out My Spirit on all flesh;
Your sons and your daughters shall prophesy,
Your old men shall dream dreams,
Your young men shall see visions.

29 And also on My menservants and on My maidservants
I will pour out My Spirit in those days.
30 "And I will show wonders in the heavens and in the earth:
Blood and fire and pillars of smoke.

31 The sun shall be turned into darkness,
And the moon into blood, Before the coming of the great and awesome day of the LORD.

32 And it shall come to pass
That whoever calls on the name of the LORD
Shall be saved.
For in Mount Zion and in Jerusalem there shall be deliverance,
As the LORD has said,
Among the remnant whom the LORD calls."

Contact info:

Emeteria Vega
Surigao, Philippines
Caraga Region
Surfing Capital
City of Island adventure
Mining Capital of the Philippines

E-mail: **emeteria.vega@yahoo.com**

Facebook: **https://www.facebook.com/ems.vega**

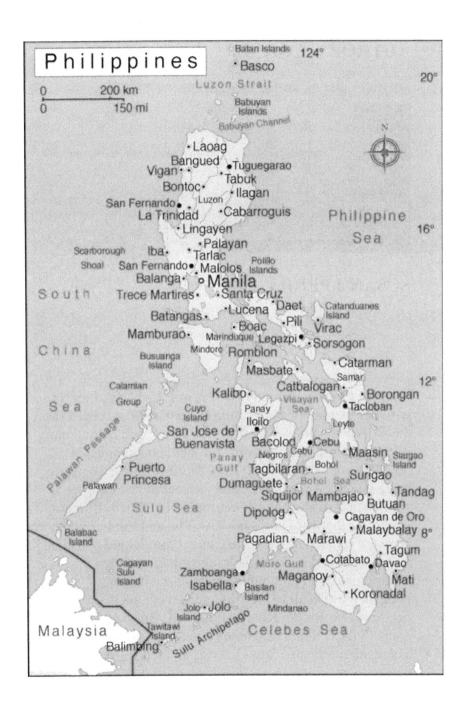

AUTHOR'S CORNER

SUSAN J PERRY

Susan J Perry currently resides in Edgewater, Florida with her blessed husband John R Perry. She is retired from the workplace but works full-time for God in many, many different ways. She prays for the sick; encourages the hopeless and writes as the Holy Spirit inspires. The Lord has given her a special lifetime project to encourage women, a task she had been crippled in all her efforts until God gave the word and said 'GO YE' and life has not ever been the same. The message came through loud and clear! Her assignment includes helping women get their testimonies in a book, published and out on the bookshelves for all to read and get saved; get healed and get delivered for the Kingdom of God. Only God could open all these doors to women's hearts to write and share. There are many amazing victories and many, many more to come!

The Bible says: *2 Timothy 4:2 Preach the word; be instant in season, out of season; reprove, rebuke, exhort with all longsuffering and doctrine.*

She and her husband continue to write and publish because now John has a significant part to play in the publishing arena. He edits; he formats, he creates the cover and produces the books and covers all the publishing bases. They are a true team for Jesus as they had always promised to be. The process is so much easier since John joined into this work because he understands by the Holy Spirit what is needed. God is so amazing throughout this couple's journey together and certainly this one is another miracle which keeps flowing into the hope of glory in Christ Jesus…

Each book brings new revelation in the word and a closer walk with Jesus as well. New friends write their stories and it's so amazing what God has done in their lives. One of their favorite scriptures comes alive because God has continued to do this for them, which is:

John 10:10 "The thief cometh not, but for to steal, and to kill, and to destroy: I am come that they might have life, and that they might have it *more abundantly."*

They do have four grown children together and they are located all over this great country; their children and grandchildren cause various vacation trips to happen wherever the need may be and the invitation occurs. They love visiting their families and continue to travel here and there, wherever God calls them to go. God has given them the abundant life as in John 10:10, with no doubt. Go ahead and find Susan J Perry books on **www.amazon.com** today.

https://www.amazon.com/s/ref=nb_sb_noss_2?url=search-alias%3Dstripbooks&field-keywords=Susan+J+Perry

Beautiful Things

Ecclesiastes 3

Everything Has Its Time

1 To everything there is a season

A time for every purpose under heaven:

2 A time to be born,
  And a time to die;
A time to plant,
  And a time to pluck what is planted;

3 A time to kill,
  And a time to heal;
A time to break down,
  And a time to build up;

4 A time to weep,
  And a time to laugh;
A time to mourn,
  And a time to dance;

5 A time to cast away stones,
  And a time to gather stones;
A time to embrace,
  And a time to refrain from embracing;

*6 A time to gain,
    And a time to lose;
A time to keep,
    And a time to throw away;*

*7 A time to tear,
    And a time to sew;
A time to keep silence,
    And a time to speak;*

*8 A time to love,
    And a time to hate;
A time of war,
    And a time of peace.*

9 What profit hath he that worketh in that wherein he laboureth?

10 I have seen the travail, which God hath given to the sons of men to be exercised in it.

11 **He has made everything beautiful in its time**. *Also He has put eternity in their hearts, except that no one can find out the work that God does from beginning to end.*

Amen.

Try choosing God's way in everything because in the book of John of the Bible it tells us:

John 14:6 Jesus saith unto him, I am the way, the truth, and the life: no man cometh unto the Father, but by me.

Jesus is the one and only way we can get to the Father or go to Heaven; the one and only way we may be saved. Salvation is only through Jesus Christ our Lord. While the world is saying many other things, our Bible says this:

Acts 2:21 And it shall come to pass, that whosoever shall call on the name of the Lord shall be saved.

Please call upon the Lord's name today and be saved. Come let us go to Heaven together when the time comes. Please don't miss out. Say this prayer after me:

"Dear Heavenly Father,
Please come into my heart and forgive my sins;
Jesus I want you to be my Lord and my Savior. Today I give my life to you. I believe Jesus died and was crucified for me and was resurrected on the third day and now is seated at the right hand of the Father making intercession for us today. Thank You for changing my life. Amen."

2 Peter 3:9 The Lord is not slack concerning his promise, as some men count slackness; but is longsuffering to us-ward, not willing that any should perish, but that all should come to repentance.

GOD'S WAY: He wishes that not one should perish but He will not go against any person's will. If he or she is adamantly against knowing the LOVE of God, He will not force you but our choices are not pleasant. Please believe me when I say that hell is real and is not a pleasant place to contemplate but when you think about eternity it is not a joke, it's forever! God will not be mocked but draws us all unto Him so we can have Heaven all our days. It is a promise you will see when you meet and accept Jesus. It is such a beautiful thing to do when you actually first accept Jesus into your heart. He loves us so much!

I can still remember my first time, it was the Fall of 1998 I asked Jesus to come into my life. My life has been so awesome ever since. I have never ever been the same and as I can continue to stand and testify with so many others:

"He is good, oh yes He is good! "

Come and receive Him today won't you? You will never live to regret it and everything will seem so much more beautiful in it's time and love will surround you like a shield. God bless you today and as you go, go with Jesus in your heart, so that your life too may be full, full of the sweet things of God.

Pursue God today!

References

1. Song: Permission for a song used in test: Miss Perry, not sure if this was ever properly answered. We would like to give you permission to use the song What a Healing Jesus in your book. This is a word that we believe should be heard. Thank you for using the title and putting it in print. Blessings to you, Dean and Mary Brown.

2. Song: Permission Request Submission

> Date Submitted: May 6, 2016
> Tracking Number: PR0319483
> Request Type: Lyric Usage
> Song Title: Through It All
> Songwriters: Brown, Gary Victor / Harve

We would like to publish a few lines of this song in our upcoming book of Women's Testimonies titled: The Persistent Widow Testifies by Susan J Perry. One woman says this song she played over & over helped her after her divorce.

*** The women who authored their testimonies in our books used various translation versions of the Bible. We have had no personal choice in which versions they used. We left that up to the discretion of each author and would like to state so here. To God be all the glory!

Made in the USA
Columbia, SC
03 July 2018